the american
blues guitar

the american
blues guitar

rick batey

A QUARTO BOOK

PUBLISHED BY
Hal Leonard Corporation
7777 West Bluemound Rd
P.O. Box 13819
Milwaukee, WI 53213 USA

Trade Book Division Editorial Offices:
151 West 46th Street, 8th Floor
New York, NY 10036

Visit Hal Leonard online at www.halleonard.com

International Standard Book No.: 0-634-02759-X

Library of Congress Control Number: 2003103936

First Edition

10 9 8 7 6 5 4 3 2 1

QUAR.BLGU

CONCEIVED, DESIGNED AND PRODUCED BY
Quarto Publishing plc
The Old Brewery
6 Blundell Street
London N7 9BH

EDITORS **Vicky Weber, Paula McMahon**
SENIOR ART EDITOR **Penny Cobb**
COPY EDITOR **June Thompson**
PROOFREADER **Anna Bennett**
DESIGNER **Balley Design Associates**
PHOTOGRAPHER **Paul Forester**
PICTURE RESEARCH **Sandra Assersohn**
INDEXER **Diana Le Core**

ART DIRECTOR **Moira Clinch**
PUBLISHER **Piers Spence**

MANUFACTURED BY **Pica Digital Pte,** *Singapore*
PRINTED BY **Star Standard Industries Pte Ltd.,**
Singapore

contents

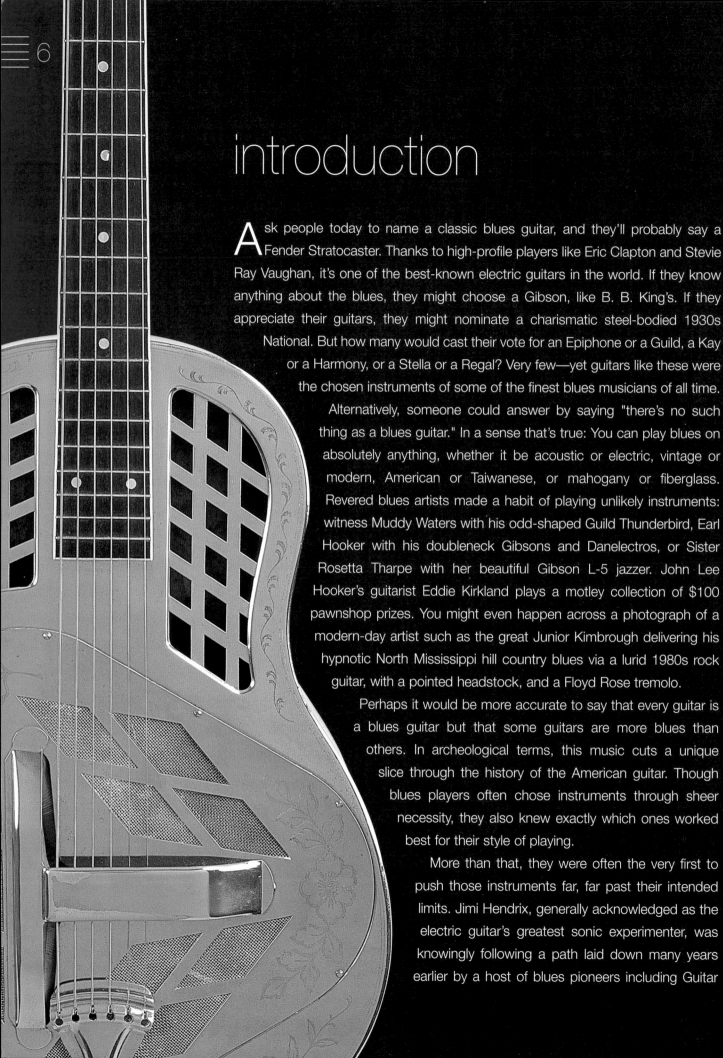

introduction

Ask people today to name a classic blues guitar, and they'll probably say a Fender Stratocaster. Thanks to high-profile players like Eric Clapton and Stevie Ray Vaughan, it's one of the best-known electric guitars in the world. If they know anything about the blues, they might choose a Gibson, like B. B. King's. If they appreciate their guitars, they might nominate a charismatic steel-bodied 1930s National. But how many would cast their vote for an Epiphone or a Guild, a Kay or a Harmony, or a Stella or a Regal? Very few—yet guitars like these were the chosen instruments of some of the finest blues musicians of all time.

Alternatively, someone could answer by saying "there's no such thing as a blues guitar." In a sense that's true: You can play blues on absolutely anything, whether it be acoustic or electric, vintage or modern, American or Taiwanese, or mahogany or fiberglass. Revered blues artists made a habit of playing unlikely instruments: witness Muddy Waters with his odd-shaped Guild Thunderbird, Earl Hooker with his doubleneck Gibsons and Danelectros, or Sister Rosetta Tharpe with her beautiful Gibson L-5 jazzer. John Lee Hooker's guitarist Eddie Kirkland plays a motley collection of $100 pawnshop prizes. You might even happen across a photograph of a modern-day artist such as the great Junior Kimbrough delivering his hypnotic North Mississippi hill country blues via a lurid 1980s rock guitar, with a pointed headstock, and a Floyd Rose tremolo.

Perhaps it would be more accurate to say that every guitar is a blues guitar but that some guitars are more blues than others. In archeological terms, this music cuts a unique slice through the history of the American guitar. Though blues players often chose instruments through sheer necessity, they also knew exactly which ones worked best for their style of playing.

More than that, they were often the very first to push those instruments far, far past their intended limits. Jimi Hendrix, generally acknowledged as the electric guitar's greatest sonic experimenter, was knowingly following a path laid down many years earlier by a host of blues pioneers including Guitar

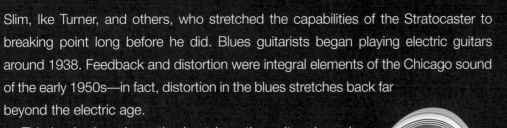

Slim, Ike Turner, and others, who stretched the capabilities of the Stratocaster to breaking point long before he did. Blues guitarists began playing electric guitars around 1938. Feedback and distortion were integral elements of the Chicago sound of the early 1950s—in fact, distortion in the blues stretches back far beyond the electric age.

This book, then, is partly about how the guitar shaped the blues: it's also about blues musicians, and how they shaped the guitar. It's impossible to overestimate how much the blues has impacted upon the popular music of the twenty-first century, and yet it has never been truly part of the mainstream. Even today, if you dedicate yourself to playing blues, you're setting foot on a steep and rocky path. For every blues guitarist mentioned in these pages, many more, just as great, were never discovered or recorded.

But musicians themselves know where the credit lies, and they can take strength from the struggles and achievements of those who have climbed this way before. Buddy Guy, at a point in his life when he had no record contract, was asked whether he ever got sick of waiting for blues to come back into fashion. "I'm not discouraged at being a blues player," he replied. "I've gone too far to turn around and say 'forget the blues'. Blues and spiritual, those are the roots of everything, of all the music being played today. I got that from the people who are no longer with us. This is not me talking, this is a relayed message. Sometimes it seems that blues players get the least of everything, but what am I going to do? I lived the life with those people. They left something behind them, and I'm just trying to carry it on."

Rick Batey, *London, 2003*

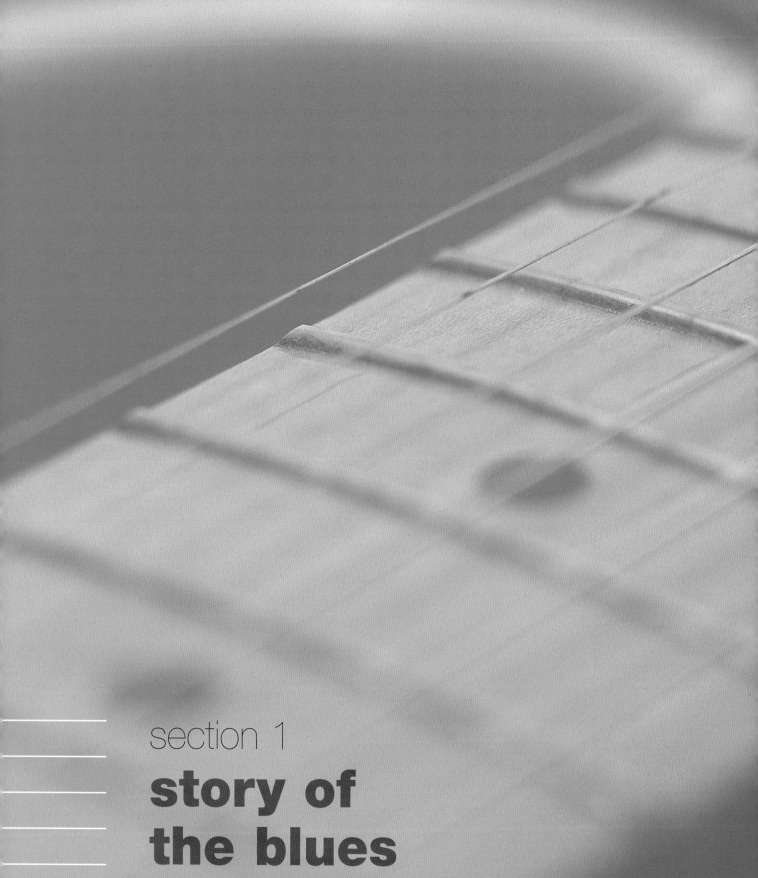

section 1
story of
the blues

from the delta to the world
an early history of the blues

"The blues was born between a man and a woman. It depends on women and men. It's about love and it's about jealousy. The blues was born when the world was born. It's about being human." Thank you, Mr John Lee Hooker. It's a statement that sums up the blues' universal appeal and neatly sidesteps all the troublesome social and political history. He's also right, of course: in the same way that relationships are the great unknown, blues is the great musical unknown.

The truism that "the blues came from Africa" is a generality that masks a complex web of interconnecting influences. The blues *did* come from Africa, but Black American music as played in the southern states, the cradle of blues music, was both a continuation of a multi-stranded tradition and a living, ever-changing response to conditions of extreme hardship. Before slavery was officially outlawed by the Americans and British in 1807, slaves were taken from many points on the west coast of Africa: the Gambia, Senegal, and the area known as the Slave Coast, including Nigeria, Sierra Leone, Liberia, Ghana, and Cameroon. In many parts of Africa, community singing and complex percussion playing accompanied every part of life, from religious ceremonies to work to celebrations, and these musical traditions impacted directly upon the development of blues.

close to the spirits

There are many connections to be drawn between the role of blues singers and that of the griots, that special caste of singers and musicians who played a vital part in many African communities' oral history. Griots had the power to act as spiritual conduits and were widely admired and rewarded, yet their special abilities also placed them dangerously close to spirits that were evil as well as good (the young Muddy Waters once saw Robert Johnson playing on the street and freely admitted being afraid to approach because of Johnson's palpable aura of danger). In some African rituals, tribespeople wear masks and adopt the entire persona of the mask's spirit, including disguising their voices. In the music of many early blues singers you can hear unearthly falsetto whoops and guttural false bass growls that may have an origin in these masked rituals.

right > **The droning bass and call-and-answer melodies of African kora players are echoed in the open-tuned guitar styles of many Delta blues guitarists.**
below > **Though it lacks a shortened "peck string," African instruments like this xalam are the direct ancestors of the unfretted 19th century banjo, the original African-American folk instrument. From the Peter Szego Collection.**

Instrumentally, too, the parallels are revealing. Musical notes themselves could be honed to the point of precise meaning—as demonstrated by the talking drum, whose changeable pitch constituted an entire percussive language. The Senegalese in particular possessed a wide range of multi-stringed instruments; the banjo, the original African-American instrument, is almost certainly the descendent of the Wolof tribe's five-string "banjer," which was played in a "frailing" style still echoed today in American folk and blues banjo and guitar styles. Listen to a skilled player of the harplike African kora and you'll hear flurries of polyrhythmic melody notes over a pulsing bass drone, and singing that bends and wavers around the third of the scale—a totally different approach to that of the artificially tempered Western scale, which has strict rules governing the use of major and minor thirds.

field hollers

Once in America, slaves were not allowed access to their traditional instruments. Drums were widely banned, as were horns, for fear that they could be used to call the people to revolt (despite this, a unique form of "fife and drum" playing exists in some rural Mississippi locations to this day). Repression can never stamp out communication: all it does is create a code, a way of saying the unsayable. Black work songs or "field hollers" might have eased the ache of spending twelve hours with a hoe under the sweltering sun, and their loose call-and-answer structure

certainly gave the blues its simple yet concentrated repetitive lyrical phrases. Yet the words themselves must have been chosen with care so as not to raise the ire of a watching overseer.

In the same way, blues lyrics are rarely overtly political: the message lies between the lines and in the singer's delivery. A complex double language was born out of slavery, and it survived long beyond abolition. A lighthearted lyric from the 1930s, for instance, may seem largely to consist of a jumble of unrelated numbers. No one but an insider would understand that each number had a very specific meaning, and that these meanings could be used to "translate" last night's dreams in order to select lucky numbers for a lottery. This gave a street-singer a way of singing loudly about extremely risqué subjects without any more danger of arrest than usual. Blues is not, by definition, despairing: it can be joyful, vengeful, historical, philosophical, loving, murderous, or a siren call to drinking, dancing, and having an all-round wild time—the full panoply of expression.

early blues

The known history of the blues goes back almost exactly 100 years, but it's almost certain that the earliest recorded blues singers/guitarists like Charley Patton and Sylvester Weaver were

left > **Cotton harvest in Georgia in the 1920s. The backbreaking work was shared by all the family.**

left > **Workers' housing on a cotton plantation in the early part of the twentieth century. The sharecropping system could leave entire communities in debt to the landowner.**
below> **With two banjos, a fiddle, a guitar, and some boards for dancing, a jug band provides the entertainment on a Mississippi plantation in the 1920s.**

not inventors but developers of a style that had been simmering for decades. Patton learned from a never-recorded singer-guitarist called Henry Sloan, a musician at Dockery's plantation near Cleveland, Mississippi. Who was he, and who was the mysterious Ike Zinneman, who reputedly taught Robert Johnson how to play? No trace remains except in the styles of their students, who were lucky enough to come of age in the era of the recording angel. Their identities are as clouded as that of the ragged-dressed stranger described in the autobiography of W. C. Handy, who recalled waiting at the station in Tuwiler, Mississippi, one afternoon in 1903 and hearing a musician passing the time by singing the eerie, repeated line "Goin' to where the Southern cross the Dog" while accompanying himself on slide guitar.

Though Handy himself was black, and a professional musician, he had never heard a guitar sounding like this, nor could he understand the words. The musician explained that his impenetrable phrase simply referred to a

point where two railroads—the Southern and the Yazoo And Mississippi Valley, popularly known as "the Dog"—crossed each other. This loading of imagery, this weighting of surface meaning, can have an immense effect upon the listener, and W. C. Handy knew a good thing when he heard it. Though blues was even then an underclass of music, rejected by the God-fearing, sung mainly by the itinerant and the near destitute just like that nameless singer at the station, Handy decided to borrow the tunes, apply his professional brush, and adopt them as his own.

Handy's "Memphis Blues" was published in 1912; the hugely successful "St Louis Blues" followed in 1914. The first-ever blues record was Mamie Smith's "Crazy Blues" of 1920, which followed Handy's brass band-influenced template and set the scene for a number of big-selling blues women singers over the next few years, including Ma Rainey, Bessie Smith, and Victoria Spivey. In his compositions, Handy was wise enough to recognize and retain the mesmeric power of the overheard "AAB" lyric format—a single line repeated twice, then topped by a rhyming punchline—but his

left > **Empress Of the blues Bessie Smith, the finest and most successful woman blues singer of the 1920s.**
right > **Country singer Jimmie Rodgers was one of the very first to incorporate blues styles into white popular music.**

single most significant legacy was the standardization of the 12-bar format, a circle of tonic, dominant, and subdominant major chords. In contrast, country blues musicians would instinctively bend and warp structure and rhythm to suit their needs: one chord, two chords, three chords…and any number of bars, depending on the lyric and the mood of the performer, but with a fascinating tendency toward thirteen or thirteen-and-a-half created by the guitar echoing two-and-half bar vocal lines. It's a freedom that survived in the music of such artists as John Lee Hooker, Robert Pete Williams, and Lightnin' Hopkins. "Lightnin' change when Lightin' want to," quipped Hopkins; it's also a treat, if a painful one, to listen to the hapless guest bassist on any number of Hooker's 1960s or 1970s recordings as he struggles to anticipate when the master will deign to shift to the IV chord.

selling the blues

The "commercialization" of blues, then, goes back a long, long way. Even as early as 1920, a fixed, rigid structure was evidently considered to be far more safe and saleable by the record companies than the dangerously wayward and possibly morally reprehensible rhythms of country blues. Today, blues lovers may sigh at the use of blues in TV advertisements selling everything from jeans to cola, but traveling medicine shows provided an important public stage for musicians, even in the early twentieth century. In the same way, radio shows of the 1930s and 1940s used musicians like B. B. King to advertise everything from cornmeal to hair products—and since these shows gave artists an opportunity to plug their show that night, the chance was invariably grabbed with both hands. B. B. King once gave a young guitarist a piece of advice: "If you're black, and you play the blues, you need all the publicity you can get." Little more needs to be said.

Influences, however, cut both ways: white musicians were influenced by black music, but the reverse was also true. The harmonies and instrumentation of Western religious music seeping into black communities' singing and playing, and, outside the church, the boundaries between African-informed blues and white folk music imported from Ireland and Scotland were

sometimes so blurred as to virtually disappear. Back in 1965 the young bottleneck player John Hammond met Howlin' Wolf, who grabbed his guitar and played an inch-perfect version of Charley Patton's "Pony Blues": "Charley Patton taught me to play that tune," growled the Wolf, "and if I screwed up, he'd whup me upside my head. I had to play it *right*!" Howlin' Wolf revealed that one of his biggest early influences had been Jimmie Rodgers, a white country singer/guitarist known as "The Singing Brakeman" who had been popular in the late 1920s. "Man, I wanted to yodel, and all I could manage to do was howl," said the Wolf. "But that guy played a lot of blues. He'd listened to Blind Lemon Jefferson and all that. Yep, Jimmie Rodgers—that's who I styled myself after." Hammond, a dedicated blues student, recalls that this information made the hair stand up on the back of his neck.

the golden age

The period from 1925 to 1929 was the age of the first true blues stars. Men such as Charley Patton and Blind Lemon Jefferson enjoyed considerable fame. Significantly, these musicians played in a tough, personal, undiluted style, the only compromise being to tailor their songs to fit on a 78 r.p.m. record. Though unable to play the theater and concert hall circuit, Blind Lemon Jefferson's records sold hundreds of thousands of copies; he traveled widely, bought cars and employed chauffeurs. Jefferson's "blind" sobriquet, incidentally, was shared by many other early country blues musicians for the most obvious and brutal of reasons: without support a visually impaired African-American could simply die of starvation, and music was one of the few ways in which he could compete on a level playing field. It's said that Blind Willie Johnson could distinguish a dime from a nickel by the sound it made landing in the tin cup wired to the head of his guitar.

Jefferson's sophisticated guitar style blazed a trail for T-Bone Walker and B. B. King. As early as 1917, he was laying the foundations for a recognizable Texas guitar style, with a strong, marching thumb-driven bass that often halted at the end of lines, while quicksilver single-note runs and turnarounds echoed the melody of the vocal. Though Robert Johnson would later record in a hotel room on his way through Dallas, Texas was no blues center. Many early players who learned their skills in the Lone Star state soon grabbed a train to ply their trade elsewhere to Chicago, Cincinnati, Kansas City, or more often west to Los Angeles.

the delta: heart of the blues

Instead, the undisputed heart of the blues lies in the Mississippi Delta. Today, this crushingly flat landscape still has the richest soil and some of the poorest economic situations in the whole of America. In the early years of the twentieth century it was the site of many huge plantations, owned by whites but mostly worked by blacks under the "sharecropping" system—in effect a glossed-over form of forced labor. Families existed on cash advances loaned by the bosses in exchange for a proportion of the profits when the crop was harvested. A poor year would yield little or no profit, and since workers were required to purchase all their goods at the plantation's own company store, many thousands of people were trapped in conditions of irreparable debt. In these large, isolated communities, cut off from electricity and outside influences, the blues took shape. Guitars, available for a few dollars, became the people's portable pianos, played in front rooms, on porches, and at weekend gatherings.

above > **A sharecropping family outside their log cabin in Mississippi, 1920s. Without electricity or phonographs, singing and playing music was an integral part of life.**
right > **Skip James, born in Mississippi in 1902, was one of the finest and earliest recorded bluesmen. His "Devil Got My Woman" was adapted by Robert Johnson.**

The guitar was ripe for the blues, the blues was ripe for the guitar, and the Delta became a crucible for an unsurpassed flowering of talent: Charley Patton, small in stature yet a rough-voiced guitar-pounder with a towering charisma; Son House, a savagely effective singer and bottleneck player. In their footsteps would follow the dexterous, falsetto-voiced Skip James; Robert

Left> **Two blues guitar greats, Mississippi John Hurt and Fred McDowell, both pictured during the blues revival years of the 1960s.**

above > **"Colored only—police order." Even after the war total segregation was still commonplace in the South, as shown by the sign on this country store in Florida in 1945.**

Johnson, raised in the phonograph age, who would synthesize imagery and guitar technique into a still unsurpassed whole; the hard-driving slide player Bukka White; the deep, complex guitar stylist Mississippi John Hurt; and the superb Mississippi Fred McDowell, who remained inexplicably unrecorded until the 1960s. That's not to say that acoustic blues did not thrive elsewhere. Over in Memphis, guitar blues was practiced by Robert Wilkins and Furry Lewis. The Piedmont, the area in the southeast reaching from Richmond, Virginia to Atlanta, Georgia, became home to a distinctive blues guitar style with a tight, danceable structure, often characterized by a subtle alternating bass played simultaneously with a ragtime-influenced melody. Blind Blake, Blind Boy Fuller, slide players Blind Willie McTell and Kokomo Arnold, and the little-known 12-string king Barbecue Bob were consummate musicians, and their verve and skill still shines clearly through the crackle and hiss of primitive recordings.

During the two decades preceding World War Two, blues was far from the only music played on the streets and in the juke-joints in the southern states. The haphazard collectives known as "jug bands" or, later, "hokum bands" were only occasionally placed before a microphone, yet they provided sterling entertainment for many years. The music of combos like the Mississippi Jook Band and The Memphis Jug Band mixed clattering boogie tunes with material lifted from traveling minstrel show tunes, played in a style that resembled proto-jazz or primal skiffle. The assortment of instruments used in jug bands was wide, to say the least. Washboards, spoons, and tambourines drove the rhythm while kazoos, harmonicas, or violins took the lead, backed up by banjos and assorted home-improvised stringed instruments, and the "jug" that gave the bands their name, a pseudo-tuba created by blowing rhythmically across the opening of an earthenware jar.

songsters

Jug bands were eventually swept away by the emergence of sophisticated solo country blues performers, and by sweeter-sounding swing bands with proper brass sections, but their anything-goes attitude toward pop and novelty songs lived on in the repertoires of many blues Even Robert Johnson, supposedly the deepest of deep blues practitioners, included light entertainment tunes like "They're Red Hot"—outwardly a tribute to a lady's tasty cooking, in fact an appreciation of her more personal talents—among the

few dozen tracks he recorded. Perhaps the best representation of the real spread of blues among most popular singer/guitarists of the time lies within the work of the "songsters" whose careers survived into the 1950s and 1960s: Mance Lipscomb, Leadbelly, even Mississippi John Hurt, and Josh White—a mixture of storytelling, folk songs, blues, and recycled vaudeville material.

gospel and the devil's music

Jazz and ragtime were also hugely popular during the 1920s and 1930s, and though the advantage of volume lay with the piano players of the day, guitarists soon found a way to play piano-style guitar with a strong alternating bass and jaunty syncopated melodies. The Reverend Gary Davis, a New York street-singer,

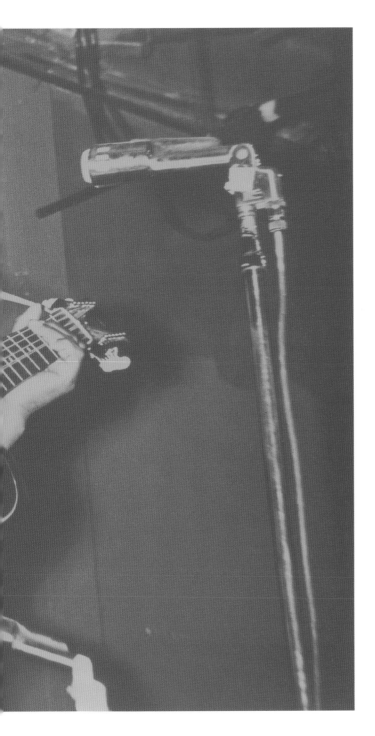

carried this tradition forward into the 1960s, and before long a new generation of pickers were transcribing complex Scott Joplin rags for the steel-string guitar. Gospel songs were also widely played by singer-guitarists, yet the schism between gospel and blues ran deep. Delta guitarist Son House, in his later years, would recount how his wife allowed him to play spirituals in the house, but consigned him to the porch whenever one of his young blues guitar students came round. It's a shock to hear the recordings of a man like Blind Willie Johnson, who played perhaps the most elegant slide blues guitar of all time but sang in a terrifying bass voice of hell and redemption.

Everything changed when the Depression struck in 1929. Phonograph discs had never been cheap: now, faced with a choice between buying Skip James' "22-20 Blues" and a loaf of bread, any hungry soul would be forgiven for grabbing the latter. A radio, on the other hand, cost nothing beyond the price of the receiver...and before long, recording companies began to sign the acts they heard on the airwaves instead of going out and canvassing new, undiscovered talent. Thus the radio clawed its way upward on the ruins of the phonograph's first golden era, and within a handful of years a rich seam of personal, localized culture had been almost entirely lost. In contrast to Blind Lemon Jefferson in the 1920s, blues artists of the 1930s such as Blind Willie McTell and Robert Johnson were completely unknown across the South as a whole. Instead it fell to a few big names, primarily Big Bill Broonzy, to represent blues in the "race" charts of the time, while a fine slide player like Tampa Red was reduced to selling simplistic double entendre material like the infamous "It's Tight Like That." Listening to the radio as the US prepared to enter the war, it may have seemed likely that folk blues had already gone the same way as the jug band and the mandolin orchestra.

left > **Street singer Blind Gary Davis became the Reverend Gary Davis in 1937, and after that usually restricted his repertoire to gospel and spiritual numbers. One of the finest blues and ragtime fingerpickers around, he taught a number of famous students including Ry Cooder, David Bromberg, Stefan Grossman, and Jefferson Airplane's Jorma Kaukonen.**

the second great blues explosion

After the war, America needed good times. Jump blues was one solution: a heady, lighthearted, saxophone-crammed cocktail of jazz, swing, and genial come-on-let's-party vocals. The jump blues sound had been shaped in the late 1930s, when large orchestras had been forced to cut back to small, maneuverable proportions. Count Basie, Louis Armstrong, Cab Calloway, and Louis Jordan were the jump pioneers, but T-Bone Walker became its first guitar star. Walker knew his blues: he'd learned first-hand from a master, Blind Lemon Jefferson. He also knew his jazz, having run with Charlie Christian before his friend found fame playing electric guitar with Benny Goodman. Walker operated out of Los Angeles, where a number of small labels—Specialty, Aladdin, Modern—had sprung up after wartime restrictions on the shellac needed to press records had ceased around 1947. Jump blues blurred the boundaries, and for the next few years hit single after hit single from the likes of Amos Milburn, Wynonie Harris, and Eddie Cleanhead Vinson mixed and matched elements from jazz, pop, piano boogie-woogie, and more—a path that would ultimately lead via a country detour at Elvis Presley and to rock'n'roll.

sweet home chicago

But there were already signs of a new down home blues revolution. Down in Helena, Arkansas, Sonny Boy Williamson III's daily "King Biscuit Time" show on radio KFFA was a proving-ground for young players like guitarist Jimmy Rogers, harpist Little Walter, and slide master Earl Hooker. In 1947 Lightnin' Hopkins released a rocking song called "Short Haired Woman," and had a hit—at least in Texas.

left > **T-Bone Walker, the father of electric blues, pictured in 1943 with his Gibson ES-250 guitar.**

right > **Sharp dressed men: guitarist Little Bill Gaither, pianist Memphis Slim, and, on the right, Big Bill Broonzy with an early National electric guitar and amp, Chicago, early 1940s.**

Then in late 1948 came the big one, John Lee Hooker's "Boogie Chillen," a shatteringly primal tune recorded in Detroit that was soon blasting out of every jukebox across the entire South. Yet the geographical center of the new blues sound was announced by Muddy Waters with the scything slide work and slap bass of "I Can't Be Satisfied." Chicago's factories had become a key destination for employment-seekers from Mississippi and the South, and Muddy Waters took control. Before long, Chicago blues—with its hollering, declamatory vocals, pounding piano, whooping amplified harmonica, gutsy, rocking rhythm sections, and fabulously gnarly yet state-of-the-art electric guitar playing— would come to be seen by the outside world as *the* blues.

right > **John Lee Hooker and old Blondie, his Epiphone Broadway, rocking the crowds with his countrywide hit "Boogie Chillen."**
below > **Good time: jazz dancers in Chicago, 1940s.**

above > **The mighty Muddy Waters band in Chicago, 1954, with Otis Spann on piano and Jimmy Rogers, right, on guitar.**
left > **Blues giant: Howlin' Wolf on stage at Silvio's club in Chicago, early 1960s.**

Chicago's rise as a magnet for workers from the South, the rise of a new, rollicking blues scene, an explosion in small black-oriented record labels, a healthy sprinkling of jumping clubs on the city's South and West Sides, and the development of the first real designed-for-business electric guitars all collided at one point in time. Before the war St Louis and Memphis had been considered bigger blues towns, but it was in Chicago that Muddy Waters—and Howlin' Wolf, Elmore James, and Robert Nighthawk—rocked up the original Mississippi blues for a new urban generation. Muddy Waters, however, was the true catalyst. He knew Friday night revelers wanted real, rocking blues, the kind they'd heard back home. He realized the key to getting club gigs was to amplify his guitar, and fast. He banished the horns, brought in a drummer and a second lead guitarist in the shape of Jimmy Rogers, highlighted the piano playing of Otis Spann, and encouraged Little Walter to amplify his harmonica. Muddy Waters' declamatory, high-voltage style could blow any band off stage, and his influence spread fast. Chester Burnett emerged as Howlin' Wolf, with a knock-'em-dead stage routine marrying the Delta

growl of Charley Patton with a rocking Memphis beat. Though Waters offered the Wolf his first Chicago gig, the two were soon locked into a bitter competition that would endure until Howlin' Wolf's death in the mid 1970s.

If the late 1920s had been the first great blues explosion, Chicago in the early 1950s was the second—but the musicians themselves made scarcely any more money than they would have thirty years earlier. Songwriting credits were openly hijacked by the record companies, while the subject of the all-important publishing royalties was simply hushed up. At least the publicity of being played on every jukebox meant there was a living to be made out touring, or else playing residencies in the city's jumping club scene. "You could go walking five blocks on 42nd Street, up 43rd or up 63rd Street and you just couldn't see all the bands that were playing on one night," recalls Buddy Guy, the hot-playing youngster whom Muddy Waters had taken under his wing after a hungry first three days in town by force-feeding him a salami sandwich. "None of these clubs closed before four or five on a Sunday! There was the Muddys, the Wolfs, then the guitar players—Hubert Sumlin, Wayne Bennett, Pat Hare with B. B. King. You'd go into some corner joint and hear three or four guys who were just as good players as any you'd ever seen, but they never made a name for themselves: that's the way it was."

the west side sound and the british blues boom

While the world was discovering rock'n'roll, Chicago blues took another turn—away from the raw powerhouse feel of Elmore James and Little Walter toward the subtler "West Side" sound. The bands changed, dropping the harmonica and adopting sax sections and electric bass in imitation of the B. B. King band. King's lyrical, emotive single-string lead playing, and soulful, impassioned vocal style was eagerly embraced by Otis Rush, Buddy Guy, Freddie King, and Magic Sam, and the development

left > **Riley "Blues Boy" King's guitar advertises one of his early radio shows in Memphis, 1948. B. B. King's style provided a template for a new generation of Chicago blues artists.**
top right > **Otis Rush, with right-handed Strat, playing a classic blues haunt, Chicago's Peppers Lounge, late 1950s.**
right > **The remarkable Magic Sam, one of the sharpest guitar stylists of the West Side movement.**

above > **Freddie King's catchy blues instrumentals were a huge influence on young British blues players like Peter Green and Eric Clapton.**

top right > **Alexis Korner's band Blues Incorporated served as an inspiration for The Yardbirds and The Rolling Stones.**

right > **Keith Richard, 1965. The Stones once visited the Chess studio in Chicago—and found Muddy Waters re-painting the ceiling. Fervent blues fans, the band did their best to repay the musical debt.**

of electric blues guitar playing leapt to a new, dramatic high-point.

With continuing success by artists like Jimmy Reed and John Lee Hooker, you'd hardly think that the blues needed a "revival" as the 1960s dawned, but suddenly an affluent new white audience was seeking the perceived authenticity of original folk music and re-appraising the work of songsters like Leadbelly and Woody Guthrie. In 1961 Columbia chose to release *King Of The Delta Blues Singers Vol. 1*, a compilation of original Robert Johnson

songs from the 1930s, and soon young rock'n'roll fans had joined this new market, looking for the sounds that had inspired 1950s Chicago revival bands like Alexis Korner's Blues Unlimited, John Mayall's Bluesbreakers, and The Rolling Stones. In a nice ironic twist, Muddy Waters horrified the earnest folk fans that faced him on his first 1958 British tour by turning his amps up to the customary 10 and letting rip; returning in 1962 he was careful to rehearse some old numbers and to bring an acoustic guitar along, but by this time the audience had caught up and now demanded the screaming slide Telecaster that had so unnerved the critics just four years earlier.

plucked from obscurity

Blues revisionism quickly spread and record companies busied themselves re-packaging fully-electric 1950s singles as albums containing "the real folk blues," though a new breed of blues-savvy US labels such as Charly, Ace, Yazoo, Document, and Arhoolie did far better work. No one was more surprised at this new turn of events, perhaps, than some of the original acoustic blues pioneers, who found themselves plucked from obscurity and pushed onstage at prestigious blues and jazz festivals on both sides of the Atlantic. Son House, Skip James, Sonny Terry, and Brownie McGhee, Robert Pete Williams, and many more all found wide audiences and, at long last, some decent-paying gigs.

Despite the alacrity of nouveau hardcore blues fans to decree what was and what was not "real" blues, the matter was out of

below > **Whooping harp player Sonny Terry and guitarist Brownie McGhee first joined forces in 1941, and by the 1960s had become one of the best-loved acts on the folk/blues circuit.**

their hands. By the free-for-all late 1960s, B. B. and Albert King were often playing to undiluted rock audiences. In Britain, Manfred Mann, The Yardbirds, and The Animals were spearheading a new R&B/pop/soul movement, while John Mayall's band had already spawned Eric Clapton, who was turning up the firepower with Cream; Peter Green, now of blues lovers Fleetwood Mac; and Mick Taylor, joining The Stones and replacing Brian Jones' basic Elmore James impressions with something rather more subtle.

supercharging the blues

Jimi Hendrix took matters even further. Hendrix had been immersed in his father's singles since he was a child, absorbing Waters, Hooker, Elmore James, Chuck Berry, and Slim Harpo. He admired the slick, stinging style of Albert Collins and the funky force of Albert King, and was reputedly especially fascinated by left-handers like Otis Rush (one listen to the acoustic 12-string version of "Hear My Train Comin'" will leave you in no doubt as how

Hendrix could turn up the wick on authenticity, should he choose. "Did ya think I could do that?" he cracks on the fade-out). Despite a fondness for the kind of extreme levels of fuzz and feedback that would have been barely tolerated at a recording session for Chicago's legendary blues label Chess, Hendrix was a true blues-man…yet the Mississippi Blues Archive only agreed to include his records after they had been donated by B. B. King. The US had its own blues-rock scene developing: harpist Paul Butterfield and guitarists Michael Bloomfield, and Elvin Bishop, dyed-in-the-wool blues lovers Canned Heat, Johnny Winter, and Charlie Musselwhite, and a new blues soul sister in the shape of Janis Joplin. Then there was Jimmy Page and ZZ Top's Billy Gibbons: by this point, blues shapes had become so much a part of rock guitar playing that it's impossible to draw a line.

That line was forcefully re-drawn by the appearance of a unprepossessing-looking kid from Dallas called Stevie Ray Vaughan. Borrowing heavily from many blues greats—though

left > **Jimi Hendrix covered songs by John Lee Hooker, Muddy Waters, Howlin' Wolf and many more—and his own "Voodoo Chile," "Red House" and "Hear My Train A-Comin" show that he would have been a great blues player at any point in history.**

right > **Powerhouse player: Stevie Ray Vaughan's death in 1990 robbed the world of its brightest blues star.**

mostly, it must be said, from Hendrix and Albert King—Vaughan tipped the scales from Chicago back to Texas, and, incidentally, paved the way for a crowd of bombastic plagiarists in ill-advised headgear all playing Stratocasters through the obligatory Ibanez Tube Screamers. But SRV was just one pioneer in a whole new era of sharp, savvy blues artists: Stevie's own brother Jimmie Vaughan, The Fabulous Thunderbirds, Anson Funderburgh, Johnny Copeland, Omar Dykes, Debbie Davies, Larry Garner, Joe Louis Walker, Chris Duarte, Kenny Wayne Shephard. Special mention must go to Robert Cray, a classic blues stylist with one foot firmly in the deep soul sound of Memphis.

future blues

But what's new? At many points in blues history it has seemed that everything has been done, that up and coming artists cannot break free of the tradition, and today is no different. Scratch the surface, though, and you'll find a vibrant scene, seething with possibilities. Acoustic blues is laden with bright talent: Kelly Joe Phelps, Keb' Mo', Alvin Youngblood Hart, Corey Harris, Eric Bibb. Even the timewarped sound of the slide guitar has been given fresh life by the imagination of Rainer Ptacek, Ben Harper and Michael Messer. Sampling technology has carried vintage blues sounds to new, undreamed-of audiences: think Little Axe, Beck Hansen, even Moby. Bands like The North Mississippi Allstars and The White Stripes are name-checking R. L. Burnside and Son House in the pages of the rock press. None of this guarantees another revolution in the making, but it does tell us that the blues remains as it has always been—a law unto itself.

left > **Kelly Joe Phelps' masterful lap-style playing recalls the work of the obscure slide artist Herman Johnson, plus Fred McDowell, Robert Pete Williams, Blind Willie Johnson, and Skip James.**

top right > **Alvin Youngblood Hart explores the original country blues styles of Charley Patton, Bukka White, Leadbelly, and Blind Willie McTell.**

right > **National player Corey Harris combines solid blues roots with jazz, reggae, and African influences.**

section 2
the guitar

stellas to stratocasters
the guitar and the blues

Blues Deluxe, Blues Special, Bluescaster, Bluesbird… you can't visit a guitar store in the twenty-first century without being assailed by products that claim to be blues-approved—steeped in a tradition, guaranteed to deliver the "right" sound, an authentic feel. It's marketing mojo, of course. Guitar players know full well that you can't buy soul in a bottle, but it must be working or they wouldn't keep on trying. Down at your friendly local store you can buy your favorite guitarist's limited-edition signature model guitar, you can pair it with a 45-year old vintage amplifier, you can even run that amp on "new old stock" tubes that have been marinating in a box since Elvis joined the army. Unfortunately, that little something that happens between the brain and the fingers will always mean that you'll end up sounding like you. If your all-time favorite blues guitarist played *your* guitar, even the old beat-up one in the closet, he would sound exactly like him. Trying to recreate the guitar tone found on that guitarist's best-ever album is even more of a fool's errand, since it was recorded through an obsolete ribbon microphone and a possibly malfunctioning compressor onto third-hand analog tape in a now demolished movie theater in Memphis. We know this. So why do we keep trying?

mystical connection

Maybe it's because guitars are not like other things. They're not just beautiful objects, and nor are they merely tools. Listening to music, we sometimes sense that there's a link between the player and the guitar that is being reflected in the very notes being produced, and nowhere is that mystical connection clearer than in blues playing at its best—one of the purest musical forms of

left > **This Floral Decalcomania dating from the 1930s is a medium-grade flat-top with the maker's typical slotted headstock, a floating bridge, and a tailpiece to take the tension away from the ladder-braced top.**

above > **A Sears, Roebuck catalog, 1920s. Just a few dollars could buy a serviceable guitar complete with case and tutor book.**

emotional communication. A fine player once admitted that when he picks up his late-1940s Stella 12-string, he feels as though Blind Willie McTell is sitting at his shoulder. Talking with blues guitarists, this kind of near-spiritual connection comes up time and time again.

These beyond-logic links are easy to understand if you have the opportunity to play a quality prewar guitar: an original Stella, for instance, or a Washburn, Regal, Gibson, or any one of the many affordable "house brand" instruments that filled the music sections of mail-order catalogs such as Montgomery Ward or Sears, Roebuck. There's no direct equivalent of these guitars still being made today. Both Martin and Gibson make fine replicas of the flat-top acoustics they manufactured in the 1930s, but US manufacturing costs puts these guitars in a different league. The source for budget acoustics now lies in the Far East, and though some imported guitars offer remarkable value for money, very few follow 1920s or 1930s lines. The situation for the 12-string country blues fanatic is even worse, as the tight-waisted, ladder-braced, 12-frets-to-the-body design seems to have entirely disappeared. In the same way that poorly printed 1960s psychedelic posters are now rare and sought after, bargain-basement American acoustic guitars are being rescued from the dumpster and sometimes even being played onstage.

resonator technology

The resonator guitar, that charismatic icon of the blues, is going through a boom period. Companies such as National Reso-phonic, Fine Resophonic, and Beltona have refined resonator technology and introduced a whole new range of stunning new styles, with both single-cone and triple-cone guitars available in wood, metal, and even carbon fiber. Electronics development has not only at last allowed resonator guitars to be fitted with practical built-in pickup systems, but has generated the birth of a whole new style of "hybrid" instrument carrying both piezos and magnetic pickups, plus the ability to blend the two systems for a great onstage sound. Playing an original Dobro or National is a wonderful experience, like being transported 70 years backward in time; unlike in the 1960s, though, fans of country blues

below left > **Before the first electric guitars arrived in the late 1930s, National steel instruments like this beautiful Style O were the loudest guitars available.**
left > **This cool Beltona guitar combines 1920s resonator technology, 1950s magnetic pickup design, and a modern piezo pickup in the bridge.**

greats like Son House, Bukka White, and Blind Boy Fuller can now buy a modern version with a superb sound and with a build quality far more consistent than the guitars of the 1930s.

All this activity among resonator guitar makers reflects a high level of interest in acoustic bottleneck blues styles. Mississippi Delta slide guitar is in many ways the very heart of the blues, but its very origin is a mystery. We will never know who "invented" bottleneck blues guitar playing. It may be that the concept is an extension of a homemade instrument known as the diddley-bow, consisting of a length of steel wire nailed to a box or even the side of a house, often tensioned and amplified by a tin can jammed underneath at one end. With a piece of metal or a bottle slid up and down the wire, a simple diddley-bow gives a whining, Western-scale annihilating sound with all the flattened thirds, unclassifiable sevenths, and limitless micro-tones on which blues guitar thrives. A number of early blues players have claimed that a diddley-bow was how they started out before they obtained a real guitar. On the other hand, some studies indicate that bottleneck guitar may partly be the offspring of Hawaiian-style slide guitar.

the hawaiian craze

It's a matter of hot debate, but Ry Cooder is one musician who's sure that Hawaiian lap steel and open-tuned "slack key" guitar methods had a wide impact across America, even before the turn of the century. "Traveling vaudeville acts and medicine shows were just about the only way people could see and hear and know about things outside the scope of their own towns," Cooder explains. "For some reason a lot of Hawaiian musicians played in these traveling shows—and also at the World Fairs which took place around the turn of the century. The speed with which the Hawaiian craze spread was really something—and the effects have rippled down into every local music scene in America, from the blues players to the hillbillies up in the mountains.

"When it comes to the blues, the connection is an elusive thing. There's the mystery surrounding the fact that rather than playing lap-style in the Hawaiian manner, black folks mostly turned their guitars upright and played in the Spanish position—typically inventive, but quite a departure. Myself, I personally don't think that bottleneck blues could have evolved the way it did without the Hawaiian influence. It's such a bizarre thing, sliding an object over the strings of a guitar. Who could have figured it out without some kind of influence? For instance, take Blind Willie Johnson: he was from near Dallas, and Hawaiian players would almost certainly

have visited that area. And we're also talking about the 1920s, when phonograph records were just becoming widespread—the first real window onto the rest of the musical world. They say Johnson learned slide from somebody else, but God knows whom *he* learned it from. Sadly, nobody back then thought to ask those kinds of questions."

spanish and vastopol

The subject of blues guitar tunings is worthy of a chapter in itself. Regular "flamenco" tuning or EADGBE is the most widespread guitar tuning in the world, but it's a compromise. What it does allow is easy access to both major and minor keys, plus an ability to vamp along with other instruments like the piano. In the 1920s ragtime blues pickers often used regular tuning, or sometimes tuned to the bottom E down to D, giving a stronger emphasis on the D root note. Twelve-string players of the 1920s and 1930s generally used standard tuning but commonly lowered the relative pitch to ease the strain on their instruments.

The pioneering slide players, in contrast, used a wide range of "open" tunings with the strummed open strings giving a full major chord. "Open D" or "Vastopol" tuning, namely DADF#AD, is a common blues slide tuning; DGDGBD, variously known as "Spanish" or "open G" tuning—or in Hawaiian terms, "taro patch"—is another. Some players, both bottleneck and fingerstyle, tuned to open C or CGCGC#D. Most of these systems were derived from banjo tunings. A number of traditional African stringed instruments are also tuned to full chords, with the lowest strings used as unstopped drones and the melody played on one or more of the higher strings. Interestingly, there's a widespread African tradition of deliberately adding loose pieces of metal to instruments so that they vibrate in sympathy with the strings, creating otherworldly buzzing, rattling noises. A National guitar can create a similarly haunting, metallic effect.

Blues tunings may also be deliberately off-pitch. Listening to the contemporary musician Cedell Davis, who plays challengingly down home bottleneck blues on a worn-out vintage archtop guitar, it's hard not to conclude that since his wayward tuning is

consistent, it's employed for musical effect. After all, there's a long blues tradition of unique self-invented tunings that runs all the way from Skip James to Albert King. Charley Patton reputedly tuned his Stella high, for extra carrying power on the noisy streets. Stevie Ray Vaughan tuned his Stratocaster a semi-tone flat for a meatier sound and to allow wider bends with his heavy-gauge strings. John Lee Hooker played standard tuning, but when he brought out his open A-tuned guitar everybody knew it was time for The Boogie. Ultimately, there are no rules when it comes to blues guitar tunings. It's up to the player to find his or her own path.

a whole new sound

By the end of the 1930s, the resonator guitar had met its future nemesis in the form of the amplified archtop guitar. The acoustic archtop guitar had originated with Gibson's L-5 of the early 1920s, an instrument mainly intended to be played plectrum-style, and offering maximum volume when vamping block rhythm chords in a dance band setting. Archtops were also widely used by jump blues musicians in the late 1930s, 1940s, and early 1950s, and there are signs that they too are coming back into fashion for blues—especially when fitted with period magnetic pickups.

Sincerely
Sister Tharpe

Deep-bodied semi-acoustics from makers like Gretsch, Epiphone, Gibson, Harmony, Regal, Silvertone, and Kay might not represent the last word in adaptability, but good examples have a lively, character-packed sound. They're especially interesting because they mark a watershed in the history of the guitar in the twentieth century, the point at which amplification allowed the guitar to challenge the saxophone as a solo voice.

All the limits on what a player could do with their makeshift amplified acoustic guitars were blown away by the appearance of the first solid-body electrics in the early 1950s. Amplified archtop guitars had been a compromise, low in sustain and prone to undesirable types of feedback; solid-body guitars solved both those problems, and also heralded a whole new sound. Chicago's Mississippi-born guitarists were probably the first-ever players to delight in the sound of an overdriven amp, deliberately to harness musical feedback and distortion, and they reveled in the advanced limits of solidbody Gibsons and Fenders. It's an oversimplification, but by the end of the 1950s, pickup technology had already divided players into two main camps—those who played Fenders and those who preferred Gibsons. It's a division that largely stands to this day.

The heart of the electric guitar is the pickup, a magnet surrounded by thousands of turns of fine wire. The pickup's job is

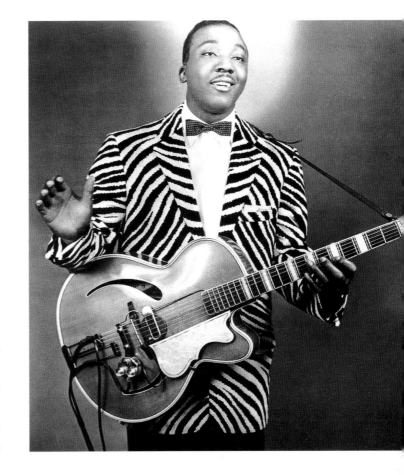

opposite page > **Sister Rosetta Tharpe, a gifted gospel/blues singer and an accomplished guitarist, with her Gibson L-5 jazz guitar.** above right > **J. B. Lenoir with a classic 1940s blues guitar—an archtop with an added DeArmond pickup.** right > **Lowell Fulson played everything from country blues, to jump, to funk. Here he's pictured with two classic Gibson blues guitars—a 1950s ES-5 and a 1960s ES-335.**

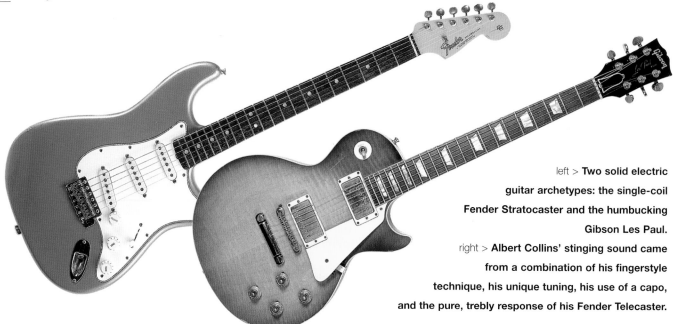

left > **Two solid electric
guitar archetypes: the single-coil
Fender Stratocaster and the humbucking
Gibson Les Paul.**
right > **Albert Collins' stinging sound came
from a combination of his fingerstyle
technique, his unique tuning, his use of a capo,
and the pure, trebly response of his Fender Telecaster.**

to turn the vibrations of the strings into electrical impulses. The role of the loudspeaker, at the other end of the chain, is the physical opposite: to change the electrical current back into vibrations. The traditional Fender pickup is a single-coil device. Being narrow, it "views" only a small section of the string. This gives a pure sound with a direct harmonic focus. It's the typical sound of modern electric Texas blues, plus a whole swathe of country and roots styles—pure and sharp. The disadvantage with the single-coil is that it's susceptible to interference, giving rise to the infamous 60-cycle hum, particularly when devices such as stage lights dimmers lie on the same mains circuit; it's a price, however, that most players are happy to pay. Gibson went a good distance toward solving the problem in 1957 by introducing a twin-coil humbucking pickup. The hum was gone, but the wider "window" viewed by two side-by-side coils gave an entirely different sound: smoother and rounder. Though Gibsons were and are widely used for blues, the humbucker's main role lies in jazz and rock. For Fender, think Otis Rush, Robert Cray, and Stevie Ray Vaughan and brother Jimmie Vaughan; for Gibson, think B. B. King, Albert King, and Freddie King.

Look closer, though, and the Fender/Gibson camps begin to blur. From the late 1930s until the late 1950s Gibsons came with single-coil pickups, most commonly the P-90. P-90s give a fatter, more mid-rangy sound than a Strat. Today, vintage replica P-90s—or humbucking pickups that *look* like P-90s and sound very roughly similar—are one of the most popular units for modern blues-oriented guitars. More complexities: from the late 1960s, some Fenders came with Gibson-style humbuckers. Albert Collins' Tele had a humbucker at the neck; Robben Ford plays a Fender Esprit, a Gibson in all but name. In the 1980s, someone had the idea of cramming a double-coil pickup into a single-coil space, giving all the advantages of hum-canceling technology while retaining a narrow field of operation and a good helping of the single-coil sound.

bending strings

There's another important difference between Fenders and Gibsons: the necks. A long 25 ½ in. scale, as found on an old Fender Stratocaster, gives a stiff, high-tension feel with plenty of "fight"; Gibson's traditional 24 ¾ in. scale makes some chords easier to reach and lets the player bend strings more easily. An old Fender's tight fingerboard radius was designed to ease the pain of playing barre chords, but it also means it's hard to set a low action without the strings "choking out"—buzzing against the frets at the high middle section of the fingerboard—when bending strings. Fender have retained a tight 7.25 in. fingerboard radius on their vintage re-issues, but most of their output now has now shifted to a middle-ground 9.5 in., retaining most of that Fender feel while allowed choke-free bending. Gibsons rarely suffered from this problem, with their gradually flattening fingerboards—from 9 in. or 10 in. in the 1930s and 1940s to 12 in. by the mid 1950s—making a fast-playing action easier to achieve.

In the acoustic field, most Gibsons have a sweet-sounding, easy-to-play 24 ¾ in. scale, which is why the J-45 and early L-0 and L-00 models are very popular for fingerpicking country blues styles. Some Martins like the 0, 00, and 000 sized models also have blues-friendly short scales; Martin dreadnought and Orchestra Model guitars have long 25 ½ in. scales, so they're harder work, yet many blues artists in the 1960s did use these guitars. On a long-scale guitar you can ease your fingers by

choosing light-gauge strings, but many current acoustic blues players prefer to play medium or heavy strings on a short-scale guitar. This "heavy is best" ethic was not always borne out by the original artists, and especially not on electric guitars. Albert Collins used light strings with an 0.009 in. on the top. B. B. King uses Ernie Ball light top/heavy bottoms, from 0.009 in. to .054 in.

Many blues players found their own personal solutions. Some reports say that as well as Gibsons and Stellas, Robert Johnson played a National with a doubled top E string for extra punch. Big Joe Williams preferred neither six-string nor 12-string guitars: his taste ran to nine or ten, with the top three or four strings doubled and the bottom two or three left single. Rather than removing strings from a standard 12-string, he would take a drill to the headstock of a six-string guitar and add several new tuners at makeshift angles. John Hammond, that fount of blues stories, has an excellent Big Joe tale from the 1960s: "I'd been driving him around from club to club," he laughs, "and late one night I went out onto the street on my own. Suddenly, *crash*—a bottle shattered on the wall just inches from my head. Some guys across the street looked like they were getting ready to start some real trouble. Just at that moment Joe appeared in the doorway, reached inside his waistband, pulled out an enormous pistol and—*boom*!—fired it straight up in the air. Those guys took off running, but man, after that, I didn't know who I should be more scared of…"

the blues guitar today

By around 1958, all the elements for what we now consider to be "the blues sound" were in place. Stella, Martin, and Gibson flat-tops, the steel-bodied resonator guitar, the Fender Stratocaster and the Fender amplifier, the Gibson ES-335; there's not much more a player of today needs to replicate the sound of almost any great blues guitarist. Amplifiers have come a long way since the 1950s, but it would be hard to argue a case for cascading-preamp technology or for digital modeling amps having much of an effect on blues in the last 20 years. In fact, the current wave of handmade vintage-style tube amplifiers is directly influenced by the great blues sounds of the 1950s and 1960s.

Equally, the designers of the best modern electric guitars have taken careful note of the golden age of the 1950s. National's much-copied Reso-Lectric guitar is basically a 40-year old solidbody-meets-resonator design, plus a single-coil pickup. Paul Reed Smith's highly rated instruments are heavily based on Gibson's Les Pauls and Les Paul Juniors, plus the personal advice of 1950s Gibson designer Ted McCarty. Fender's Telesonic guitar combines the half-century old Telecaster outline with Gibson's set-neck construction and P-90 pickups. As far as blues is concerned, carbon graphite necks, pseudo-acoustic piezo bridge technology, and onboard active electronics have pretty much rattled past on a different set of tracks. At the moment it seems that blues players aren't much interested in "the latest thing," which is not how it used to be. In the 1930s a National steel guitar must have looked as if it had landed from Mars, and if you speak with any guitarist who hung around Chicago in the late 1950s it won't be long before he enviously mentions Earl Hooker, who had some mysterious hold over the largest music store in town and was never seen without the craziest new gear in town, from doubleneck guitars to wah-wah pedals. Earl Hooker's example shows that the blues is not restricted to a particular type of guitar, to approved trade names or the exact material you choose for a bottleneck. Having a great guitar at their disposal never did anybody's music any harm…but it's the player that matters most.

left > **The unique Big Joe Williams with one of his famous home-adapted guitars, Chicago, 1947.**

above > **Gibson's long-running J-45 is regarded as one of the best flat-top acoustics for blues.**

right > **National's Reso-Lectric guitar combines solidbody and resonator sounds.**

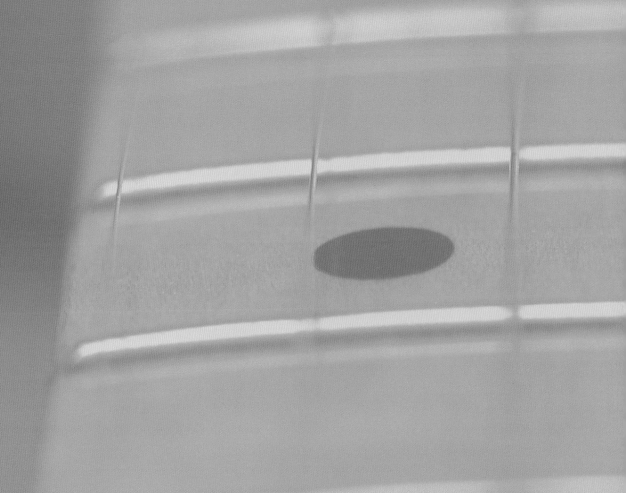

section 3
the guitars and their players

martin inventing the american guitar

Almost certainly the most important guitar maker in American history was German immigrant Christian Frederick Martin. Like many other instrument makers escaping the tough rules of the violin-making guilds, Martin emigrated to the US in 1833, where hundreds of Europeans had formed the backbone of a blossoming American music industry.

High-quality guitars were being manufactured by many companies by the mid-1800s, but Martin led the way with an innovative system of re-inforcing the top, later known as "X" bracing, a system still used on many acoustic guitars today. Martins have always been finely made guitars, and would have been the dream instrument of any player in the US between the 1850s and the early 1900s. While unaffordable for most working people in America's Deep South in the 1800s, the Martin is typical of the size and shape of guitars seen in the earliest photographs of bands playing blues.

The old European guitar had been a small, quiet, heavily decorated instrument; Martin guitars, in contrast, were all about the sound. The company defined a new body shape, more abruptly waisted and with a smaller upper bout than the old European "hourglass" design. They dropped the curved, ornate bridge for a simple, rectangular design with "pyramid" ends to help keep the top as freely-vibrating as possible. The headstock was simple, square, and austere. The bracing was re-evaluated from top to bottom in the search for added volume and better tone. And in the face of increased competition from large manufacturers of far cheaper guitars, Martin turned successfully to making fine mandolins and ukuleles and still managed to lead the way in making ever larger, better sounding guitars.

below > **Shape of things to come: This classic Martin from the gut-strung era—a Style 28 in the 1 body size—dates from the 1860s. It has rosewood back and sides and a spruce top, plus an unusual added pearl soundhole ring.**

right > **The stylish and sophisticated Lonnie Johnson, here pictured in the 1960s, was not just a country blues player: in the jazz guitar world, he's just as important a figure as Charlie Christian and Django Reinhardt.**

lonnie johnson

Though he became most famous as the first truly great jazz guitarist, Lonnie Johnson also laid down the whole future of blues guitar. Born in 1889 in New Orleans, Johnson won a St. Louis blues talent contest for eighteen weeks straight in 1925 and was awarded a recording contract with Okeh, recording an incredible 130 discs. He also laid down some amazing guitar duets with Eddie Lang, played guitar for Duke Ellington and Louis Armstrong, and was back in the limelight in the 1940s and from 1963 to his death in 1970. Johnson had swing, fluidity, and drive—even B. B. King declared him a greater influence than Robert Johnson. He played a number of guitars during his long career, including a National resonator, a Vega flat-top and, later, semi-acoustic Gibsons, but his best-known guitar was his trademark 12-fret Martin 00–21.

identifier

early martin guitars

identifying early martins—now hot collectors' items—is difficult. Martin collaborated with various others, and guitars from Nazareth, Pennsylvania also appeared with names such as Martin & Coupa, Martin & Schatz, and Martin & Bruno.

martin numbers The first part indicates the maximum body width; the second, separated by a hyphen, indicates the level of quality and decoration. Any Martin without a serial number or a model number (stamped inside, on the neck block) was made before 1898.

body width From 1840 to around 1900 Martins came in a gradually increasing series of sizes:

¼: 8 $^{15}/_{16}$ in.

½: 10 ¼ in.

3 ½: 10 $^{11}/_{16}$ in.

5: 11 ¼ in.

3: 11 ¼ in., longer 17 ⅜ in. body

4: 11 ½ in.

2 ½: 11 ⅝ in.

2: 12 in.

1: 12 ¾ in.

0: 13 ½ in.

00: 14 ⅛ in.

quality and decoration
Numbers range from 17—the plainest—up through 18, 20 to 24, 26 to 28, 30, 33, 34, 40 to 42, with a pearl-inlaid border, fingerboard, and soundhole.

top right > **This ornate, ivory-bridged "baby D-45"—the forerunner of the famous "dreadnought" design—was specially made by Martin for the Oliver Ditson store in New York around 1919.**

above right > **A pearl-decorated Martin 1-40 from the middle 1870s.**

larson and lyon and healy
the sound of steel

Martin may have been the most famous name in guitars at the turn of the century, but it fell to other makers, including Gibson and the Larson brothers, to design the first acoustic flat-top guitars designed specifically to carry that all-important ingredient of blues guitar, steel strings.

Carl and August Larson were Swedish immigrants who arrived in Chicago in the late nineteenth century. Admiring the volume of steel-strung mandolins, they set about designing guitars that would handle the extra tension with extra-strong laminated hardwood braces under the top, plus an arched top and back. With a patent granted in 1904, the Larsons set about making an imaginative range of steel-strung guitars, mandolins, and "harp guitars" under a host of different names, including Stahl, Maurer, Stetson, Prairie State, Euphonon, and others. In those days it was common practice for guitar makers to use the pulling power of a well-known local music dealer or guitar teacher to sell their wares. Larson guitars were sold in Chicago under the banner of Robert Maurer, while residents of St. Paul, Minnesota would have bought a similar guitar labeled Dyer. Some of the Larson brothers' best and most up-to-the-minute guitars were built in the mid to late 1930s under the name Euphonon, a name chosen by the makers to replace the Maurer brand.

Euphonon guitars were big and confident, and they're now achieving a high collectable status. Many of the models—such as square-shouldered dreadnoughts and Grand Auditorium designs with 14 frets to the body—echoed Martin's ideas of the time. Others were not dissimilar to some of Gibson's flat-top jumbo models, with super-large, rounded bodies. The Larson brothers died within two years of each other in the early 1940s, but left behind a legacy of some of the best-built and most forward-looking instruments in the history of the American guitar.

right > **This Larson-made Stahl guitar, made around 1910 in the old Maurer factory in Chicago, is a plain but handsome student-grade model with straight bracing instead of the more upmarket Martin-style X-bracing.**

identifier

Identifying old American steel-strung guitars can be tough, as the best makers used a huge variety of different brands—and some, like the Larson Brothers, almost always branded their guitars under other names. Here are some of the better-known variations from the first few decades of the twentieth century:

ditson of Chicago
Bay State
Haynes Excelsior
Tilton

lyon and healy of
   Chicago
Washburn
Boehm
Windsor

larson of Chicago
Maurer & Co. (early)
Stahl
Dyer
Stetson (budget Dyer
   brand)
Prairie State
Euphonon (later, often
   like Martins)
Knutson (harp guitars)

martin of New York
   and Nazareth, PA
Martin & Schatz
Martin & Coupa
Martin & Bruno
H. & J.
Paramount
Ditson

gibson of
   Kalamazoo, MI
Cromwell
Kel Kroyden
Recording King
Roy Smeck
Junior
Kalamazoo
Old Kraftsman

kay of Chicago
Kay Kraft
Mayflower
Orpheum
Recording King

regal of Chicago
Regal
20th Century
University
Bacon & Day

weymann of
   Philadelphia, PA
Weymann
Keystone State
W & S
Varsity

lyon and healy

Martin and Larson made the biggest strides in early American guitar design, but many more early blues musicians would have come across guitars made by the Chicago instrument-making giant Lyon and Healy under the Washburn brand. By the turn of the century, the company claimed to be making in excess of 100,000 Washburn instruments each year—almost a thousand times as many as Martin. What's more, Washburns were made to suit every pocket: their $200 pearl-decorated guitars were amongst the best in the country, but for as little as $10 you could buy a serviceable student-grade model.

The golden age of Washburn guitars lasted from around 1900 until 1928, when Lyon and Healy turned their back on the guitar-making business in favor of pianos and harps. The Washburn factory was sold to J. R. Stewart, who used the facility to make guitars under the Tonk Bros. name—good guitars, but plainer and less well-made than in Washburn's heyday. Today's Washburns are a completely different concern, as the famous name has been relegated to a range of instruments made in the Far East.

right > **Some old Washburns can make great blues guitars. This stenciled-top Style A with its stylish bridge design, one of the last original Lyon and Healy Washburns, dates from around 1928.**

right > **This highly decorated Washburn Style 108 dates from the 1890s.**

catalog guitars buying from the book

Catalog guitars were the instruments on which the blues was built. Musicians may have lusted after intricately crafted Martins and Washburns, but the guitars most of them played were ordered from catalogs. Away from the cities and the larger towns, a complex network of representatives toting lavishly illustrated sales literature covered the back country selling furniture, household goods, and luxury items such as musical instruments, all available at variably reasonable terms of repayment. As little as $2 or $3— a tiny fraction of the price of a Martin—guaranteed delivery of a guitar which could be played, more or less. A little more, up to $10, got you a quality instrument.

Most guitar players in the isolated regions of America's South would have plumped for the very cheapest available catalog models out of sheer necessity. Financially speaking, at anything up to $70 or $80, a top-line Martin or Washburn would have been impossibly out of reach for anyone but the most successful of musicians. Yet although affordable catalog guitars would have been manufactured in huge quantities and sometimes in a relatively rough and ready fashion, surviving examples can sound surprisingly rewarding, with a trebly but character-crammed tone.

These guitars might have been cheap, but they were also designed to last—a major advantage in the days when most working musicians' instruments had short life expectancies. Guitars in the 1920s were often strung with steel strings that would be considered extremely heavy by the standards of today, and many would have been played mercilessly hard. With thick, sturdy necks and bodies made of laminated timbers, the guitars sold by companies like Wards and Sears, Roebuck could withstand extremes of heat and humidity. They could take the rough-and-tumble of street-corner playing, cope with long nights being thrashed at dances, and survive being lashed to the back of a Model T Ford with a piece of rope—and if it didn't survive, then a few dollars would buy you another.

above > **A Sears catalog for "Supertone"
guitars, 1927.**
right > **This vibrant-sounding parlor-sized guitar
is not strictly speaking a catalog instrument, but an
Oscar Schmidt-made Stella dating from 1905. It has a
wide, v-shaped neck typical of the period.**

identifier

charley patton

Through the crackle and hiss of 78 r.p.m. vinyl comes the huge voice and pounding, syncopated guitar of Charley Patton, the founding father of Delta country blues. Born around 1887, he took up guitar in 1907 and by 1929 had become a sought-after celebrity, a vaudeville-style showman of unparalleled power who could snap from down-home blues to comedy numbers in a split second, then launch into impassioned gospel preaching.

Patton used a brass pipe as a bottleneck, and employed all the classic trickery of the street musician: the guitar-with-the-strap moves, snapping at the strings, playing behind his head. He also performed Hawaiian-style, with the guitar held flat and gripping a knife in his left hand. Patton possessed a famously strong "500-yard voice," and often tuned his Stella up higher than usual, achieving a driving, strident sound. Son House, Mississippi Fred McDowell, and Bukka White all fell under his spell: so did Robert Johnson, and later, Muddy Waters—and Howlin' Wolf's urgent 1950s sides echo were pure Charley Patton. Weakened by a life of legendary carousing and risk-taking, the dangerous entertainer succumbed to heart failure in Indianola, Mississippi, in 1934.

straight bracing

The unique guitar sound of early blues greats such as Charley Patton is inseparable from the guitars they played.

Early steel-strung guitars were "straight-" or "ladder-" braced, not with the C. F. Martin-developed X-bracing but with a system of re-inforcing struts running at 90 degrees to the grain of the top.

straight bracing allowed the top to move almost like a drum-skin, producing a great deal of volume and an open, vibrant tone.

tailpiece straight-braced tops are ill-equipped to deal with the twisting forces applied by a glued bridge, so many of these guitars were originally equipped with a tailpiece, transferring the tension of the strings down to the bottom of the guitar.

below > **This diagram shows the "straight" or "ladder" bracing pattern typical of that on a 12-string Oscar Schmidt guitar. Straight bracing makes for a super-loose, responsive top, and it gave old-time blues pickers the vibe and volume they needed straight off the shelf.**

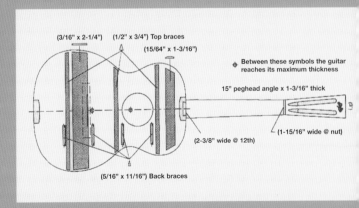

left > **The only known photograph of Charley Patton, the man who first defined the Delta blues style.**

stella guitars first choice

Stellas are the instruments chosen by the cream of original country blues pickers: Blind Blake, Blind Lemon Jefferson, Charley Patton, Blind Willie McTell, Barbecue Bob. Then there's Robert Nighthawk, Homesick James, Honeyboy Edwards, Sleepy John Estes, Furry Lewis, Rambling Thomas, Henry Townsend, Lulu Jackson, Buddy Boy Hawkins, Sam Collins and Jim Jackson all used Stellas. Stellas were easy enough to find in ordinary hardware stores, but it wasn't just a matter of convenience—many guitar players genuinely valued these guitars above any other brand for their toughness and volume.

These early, original Stellas have almost no similarities with the later Stella-branded guitars made by the giant Harmony factory in Chicago from the 1940s through to the 1970s. Some of the postwar Harmony-made Stellas are fine-sounding guitars, but their design is relatively crude. Original Stellas were manufactured by the Oscar Schmidt company of Ferry Street in Jersey City and they're more sophisticated, and of much higher quality. Oscar Schmidt was a German immigrant from Saxony—also the homeland of C. F. Martin—who founded his own company in 1879, beginning by publishing sheet music and soon moving onto a whole range of musical instruments including guitars, mandolins, banjos, autoharps, ukuleles, and zithers. By the 1920s the company was also making guitars under names like Sovereign, La Scala, and Galiano, as well as supplying instruments for other concerns under names such as Tonk, Bruno, and Sterling.

Oscar Schmidt did not sell instruments through the large mail-order catalogs; the company had its own team of salesmen, who made sure that Stella guitars were stocked both by music stores in the larger cities and also by plain general stores in the remoter rural areas. This policy paid off, and Stellas were often more popular in Mississippi and the Appalachians than Gibson guitars. Today there's a renewed level of interest in genuine Oscar Schmidt guitars. Although surviving examples often need a great deal of work to make them playable once again—neck resets, side repairs, and even larger internal bridge plates are sometimes necessary—the results are always worth it.

above > **The most expensive Stellas, like this beauty from 1925, were second to none, with solid rosewood backs and sides and ornate pearl inlays running up the fingerboard. Both Son House and Charley Patton were reputed to have played Stellas with this type of "tree of life" fingerboard inlay.**

right > **Blind Blake was probably the finest recorded fingerpicking-style guitarist of his generation. Here he's playing a regular-sized, dark-topped Stella guitar.**

identifier

blind blake

Suave, sophisticated, and holding a small-bodied, dark-topped Stella, Arthur "Blind" Blake smiles from his one surviving photograph. Blake fingerpicked his guitar in the piano style, immaculately well, with fabulous syncopation and swing: "the happy guitar of Blind Blake," as the adverts ran. Blake snapped up a record deal in 1926 and scored tremendous success with his first Paramount release, "West Coast Blues." Moving to Chicago, he recorded as a soloist and on numerous band cuts too—fabulous sessions with banjoists and clarinettists and vocalists like Ma Rainey and Ida Cox. No-one knows what happened to the man himself: he simply disappeared some time after a recording session in 1932. His compositions still challenge the dexterity of fingerstyle guitarists to this day.

New Jersey-made Oscar Schmidt guitars were very European in influence. Schmidt owned five factories in Europe and sourced his inlay materials from Germany.

size Schmidt-made Stellas came in at least four different body sizes, including three-quarter size, standard size, Grand Concert, and Auditorium. Most had plain "dot" position markers.

woods of almost every combination, including oak, mahogany, maple, and koa were used in Stellas. The vast majority were made of plain birch wood, with either a birch or a spruce top. Often the back and sides would be "faked" to resemble more expensive wood by using a feather dipped in dye.

paper labels inside and **slotted headstocks** usually featured in early OS Stellas. Later Harmony-made Stellas have no paper label and usually carry a solid headstock.

above > **In search of greater volume, Stella guitars grew gradually larger. This silvery sounding "Marquette" model was made in 1910.**

blind lemon jefferson **man-and-guitar**

The best-known image of early blues superstar Blind Lemon Jefferson shows him playing a small-bodied Stella guitar. Blind Lemon Jefferson made a living playing on the streets of Dallas—sometimes accompanied by a young T-Bone Walker—before recording his first sides in 1925 for Paramount. Jefferson's guitar style combined tough, rolling rhythms—in his words "booger rooger"—with sudden stops, before breaking into single-note flourishes which echoed the style of field hollers. His repertoire included gospel material and the first genuine man-and-guitar blues to hit a mass audience: tunes like "Corinna Blues," "That Black Snake Moan," and "Jack O' Diamonds Blues" are vital slices of early greatness, while others—"See That My Grave Is Kept Clean" and "Matchbox Blues"—were recorded in the 1960s by Bob Dylan, Carl Perkins, and The Beatles. Jefferson, born in Couchman, Texas, at a date unknown, made a fortune, but met a tragic death by heart attack after being snowed in during a long car journey in 1929.

far right > **A huge recording star in his 1920s heyday, Blind Lemon Jefferson makes his Stella guitar look like a toy. Like many bluesmen, Jefferson probably went through a large number of instruments.**

below > **This stunning Stella "Floral Decalcomania" dates from the 1930s. The black-painted body carries a fancy reflective pickguard and is edged in a gold sparkle material. The headstock carries the "underlined" Oscar Schmidt-era Stella logo and the fingerboard is made of imitation pearl. Pearloid fingerboard guitars don't always sound the best...but they look fabulous.**

stella guitars recapture the early blues

Early Oscar Schmidt flat-tops have become increasingly sought after by players, seeking to recapture the early blues sounds and styles, and collectors, fascinated by their endless variations in the construction and decoration. Some are plain; others—so-called "Decalcomania" guitars—carry colorful decals on their tops, a fashionable feature in the 1920s and 1930s.

A browse through a 1921 Oscar Schmidt wholesale catalog might find you a plain model guitar in imitation Hawaiian koa wood for just $2.75, and, for just 25 cents more, a spruce-fronted model. A simple Grand Concert-sized guitar could be bought for $3.75, while $4.75 got you an Auditorium-sized model—loud enough for any juke-joint dance. Imitation rosewood guitars sold for between $5 for plain and $8 for extra-fancy; $27 bought a spectacular contra-bass or harp guitar with an extended body, a regular six-string neck, and six extra-long bass strings.

Cordially Yours
Blind Lemon Jefferson

the age of the 12-string guitar
sheer volume

The idea behind the first American 12-string guitar probably drifted up from Mexico, where double-course guitars were well-known; but the 12-string was perfected by Italian craftsmen in the workshops of Oscar Schmidt, Regal, and Harmony. By the turn of the century, 12-string guitars were relatively common-place, with one simple advantage over conventionally strung guitars: sheer, clanging volume.

As with ordinary guitars, there were no rules about how you should string or tune a 12-string guitar. As well as standard tuning, players often chose "Spanish," open G, or "Vastopol" tuning, open E, both of which suited slide work. The steel guitar strings of this time were incredibly heavy by modern standards, at least a 0.014 in. or 0.015 in. on the top E. Often musicians would decrease the strain on their instruments by transposing open E down to open D. Many detuned even further, down to C on the bottom string, and invented new combinations of unison and octave paired strings.

Despite their volume, 12-string blues players were a rarity. By the mid 1930s the 12-string was virtually extinct, with examples found only in the catalogs of Stella of Jersey City and Regal of Chicago. It would be 30 years before the folk explosion of the 1960s re-awakened the sleeping 12-string giant. Martin would jump onto the bandwagon by the simple expedient of adding 12-string necks to their dreadnought and, later, round-shouldered dreadnought models. Gibson would provide the B-45-12, a 12-string version of their own dreadnought design. Guild's beefy-sounding jumbo guitars proved an excellent vehicle for a dozen strings. Even Fender began producing acoustic 12-strings. But prewar 12-strings have a style and a vibe all their own.

above > **This Oscar Schmidt-made 12-string was made around 1930 and was branded "San Jose" for a New York retailer called Horenstein & Sons. It has fancy herringbone binding, ornate floral neck inlays, and a fixed "pyramid" bridge.**

blind willie mctell

Atlanta 12-string guitarist Blind Willie McTell shares with Blind Blake and Barbecue Bob the reputation of being one of the finest exponents of the Piedmont blues style: jaunty, elegant, and leaning heavily toward ragtime. McTell, born blind in Thompson, Georgia, around 1900, escaped a bleak future through his musical upbringing. He traveled extensively with Blind Willie Johnson. McTell combined complex, syncopated fingerpicking and driving slide work wonderfully. He was photographed more often than most of his contemporaries, usually with a different guitar each time. In the best-known early shot, though, he carries a laminated-topped Westbrook, a brand closely associated with Stella.

He quit playing guitar in the 1920s to attend a school for the blind, where his callused fingers hampered his ability to read Braille, but soon returned to music and recorded as late as 1947. A few years after his death in 1959, McTell's "Statesboro Blues" would become a classic again in the hands of Taj Mahal and the Allman Brothers.

identifier

the 12-string guitars

This super-rare 12-string guitar—probably the only one in existence—would have been a costly instrument even when brand new in 1914. It's branded as a Weymann, but since the H. A. Weymann company of Philadelphia was mostly known for making banjos and mandolins, some experts think this guitar may have been built by their near neighbors, C. F. Martin. Though as beautifully appointed as a Martin, and built to the highest standards in spruce and Brazilian rosewood with "rope-pattern" body inlays and a long, elegant headstock, the design is unlike anything offered by Martin, with a design that routs only half the strings through to the tailpiece. This delicate and wonderful-sounding style of 12-string guitar with 12 frets to the body has all but disappeared.

Though labeled "Westbrook," this guitar was also a product of the Oscar Schmidt company. Constructed simply of all-laminated woods, this big-sounding, super long-scale 12-string is identical to a guitar played by Blind Willie McTell in an early photograph. It has a sunburst top, a simple printed soundhole decoration in place of pricier inlays, brass frets, a solid as opposed to slotted headstock, and a tailpiece to help ease the strain of a dozen thick strings. This guitar was made in the 1930s.

left > **Georgia bluesman Blind Willie McTell.**

regal ruling the 1930s

Mandolin and guitar makers Regal of Chicago hit its stride in 1931 when it acquired the well-equipped factory of J. R. Stewart. Soon Regal had vastly expanded its range to include some excellent flat-top guitars—some under the Regal name, some under the Washburn banner—plus a selection of large, handsome archtops and even an array of resonator guitars made under license from Dobro. Guitars like this spectacular Le Domino would have appealed greatly to the blues fraternity, as dominos, dice, and other games of chance and skill were hugely popular in the black community. Regal's postwar guitars just weren't the same, and eventually the name was bought by Harmony and used on a range of Fender-distributed student guitars.

Regal's range was wide. They made many different flat-tops, from six- and twelve-string to four-string tenors. Their f-hole archtops were subtle, classy Gibson-influenced guitars whilst their roundhole archtops were Martin-like. They also made cheap, funky, almost Gretsch-alike jazzers, some under the Recording King brand.

Oahu, based in Cleveland, Ohio, was another maker of fine guitars much valued in the 1930s. Oahu's guitars all came with "the new SafeTiString posts," a "special reinforced bridge," "Oahu polished strings," and the "Oahu De Luxe hand-rubbed finish." "For one who appreciates a neat looking instrument without elaborate handiwork and whose primary interest is tone quality and workmanship," boasted the company's catalog, "we recommend this instrument as the best that money can buy. It is guaranteed to last a lifetime."

top > **This hilariously named Regal Le Domino Big Boy has dominos on the belly, around the soundhole, and even up the neck. It would have been a fabulous instrument for a lead blues guitarist in the early 1930s—it sounds almost like a Telecaster.**

above > **This high-quality jumbo guitar—very big-bodied for 1927—was sold by Oahu as a genuine Hawaiian-made instrument, but in fact it was made by Kay of Chicago.**

identifier

blind willie johnson

Guitar-playing evangelist Blind Willie Johnson used the devil's instrument to do the Lord's work. With a dark, guttural voice and one of the most advanced slide guitar techniques ever heard, Johnson's music still sounds astonishing today. His songs are stark and menacing, with no humor, no relief; it's pure hellfire preaching, honed to a terrifying edge.

Born in Marlin, Texas around 1900, he was blinded at the age of seven when his stepmother, beaten up by his father after being caught in flagrante with another man, retaliated by throwing lye in the child's face. Johnson would eventually die in the 1940s of pneumonia after sleeping in a soaked bed following a fire that burned his house down. He recorded between 1927 and 1930, then moved to Beaumont, Texas where he made a living as a respected street-singer, playing for the crowds with a tin cup wired to the headstock of his Stella guitar. His greatest songs—"Dark Was The Night," "Lord I Just Can't Keep From Crying" and "You'll Need Somebody On Your Bond"—would have a huge effect on 1960s blues revivalists like Ry Cooder and Taj Mahal, while Eric Clapton named "It's Nobody's Fault But Mine" as the finest slide playing ever recorded.

prewar giants

This extra-large jumbo guitar with its beautiful decal decoration was made by Oahu around 1938. The top is spruce, the back and sides sycamore. Some of Oahu's jumbos came in both 14-fret round-neck and 12-fret square-neck format: this one is a converted square-neck. When new, this guitar would have cost a hefty $98.

Some important American guitars are hard to identify. Although thought to be a Stella, the body shape of this huge, plainly built 12-string is unlike any known Stella model—in fact, it almost looks as though it was designed to hold a resonator. It's likely that it's a prototype Regal, reputedly one of only half a dozen ever made in this style. This massive and rare instrument has pearwood back and sides and an extra-long scale.

left > **The incomparable Blind Willie Johnson, the most advanced slide guitarist of the prewar era.**

leadbelly king of the 12-string guitar

The man who single-handedly saved the 12-string guitar from going the same way as the harp-guitar was Huddie "Leadbelly" Ledbetter. Born near Shreveport, Louisiana in 1888, Leadbelly grew up in Texas and learned his guitar craft acting as a guide for Blind Lemon Jefferson. This idyllic spell ended in 1916, when Leadbelly was jailed for assault: He escaped, but was soon re-convicted and spent seven years in a Texas jail and then a stretch in Louisiana State Penitentiary, the infamous Angola.

It was in Angola in 1933 that a meeting took place that would shape the history of American folk and blues. Musical folklorist John Lomax, seeking singers who knew the old-time tunes to record for the Library of Congress, decided to visit some prisons—and in Leadbelly he discovered a powerhouse performer with a repertoire of some 500 songs. After Leadbelly was released the pair headed north to embark upon a series of lectures and demonstrations, but their relationship soon soured: The ex-convict soon became the darling of the liberal Greenwich Village set, but when Lomax booked a gig at Harlem's Apollo, black audiences proved disinterested in a man whose music seemed a full decade or more out of date.

In his later years, however, Leadbelly's New York house became a magnet for folk and blues artists both black and white, including Sonny Terry, Brownie McGhee, and Woody Guthrie. The songs he wrote—or adapted—became central to the new folk revolution: "Rock Island Line," "Careless Love," "Pick A Bale Of Cotton," and "C. C. Rider" ("Mama, Did You Bring Any Silver" even became the template for Led Zeppelin's "Gallows Pole"). Leadbelly died in 1949, just a year before folk group The Weavers made his "Goodnight, Irene" a nationwide hit.

above > **American 12-string legend Huddie "Leadbelly" Ledbetter playing his iconic Stella guitar alongside his wife Martha in the 1940s.**

sound secrets

Though Leadbelly discovered his first 12-string in a Dallas pawnshop around 1912, his most famous guitar was custom-ordered in 1935, from the Oscar Schmidt company, who had sold the rights to the Stella name in 1930 to John Carner. This big-bodied, long-scale 12-string monster was made of spruce and mahogany and sported an extra-thick white pickguard probably fitted

by the owner himself. Leadbelly tuned his guitar from C to C, a full four half-steps down from standard, and arranged his strings in an unusual way: in unison for the top three pairs of strings, in octaves for the fourth and fifth pairs, and with a double octave on the bottom C.

made in 1935 in Jersey City by Fulvio Pardini, a craftsman in the Oscar Schmidt workshop.

body 15 ¾ in. wide, made of mahogany.

top Solid spruce, ladder-braced.

neck Mahogany, built to a super-long 26 ⅝ in. scale for extra string tension and volume. Joins the body at the twelfth fret.

today 1930s Stella 12-strings are highly valued and virtually unobtainable. Players seeking to capture Leadbelly's thunderous sound often order custom-made replicas from specialist builders, such as this Leadbelly Special by Dell' Arte.

the weissenborn guitar

koa wood guitars

The American fascination with Hawaiian music began in the 1890s, exploded around 1915, and carried on well until the 1930s. Guitar historians continue to ask, was the lyrical, swooping "Hawaiian" guitar style—stopping the strings with a solid metal bar while holding the instrument flat on the lap— the main influence on blues players' widespread technique of "slide" playing while tuning their guitars to an open chord? There's no one answer. There was crossover, no doubt, but the basic fact that blues slide players generally held their guitars upright while employing a glass bottleneck (or a simple metal tube) slipped over a finger seems to point toward separate roots.

The popularity of Hawaiian guitar playing spawned a vast network of teachers, conservatories, and tutor books, and created a whole new school of guitar design. Martin and Gibson both made thousands of lap-style guitars, but perhaps the finest examples were made by German émigré Herman W. Weissenborn of Los Angeles, using exotically figured Hawaiian koa wood, with thick, square necks and extra-high nuts to raise the strings for a clean, sweet tone. Weissenborn made guitars from the 1920s until his death in 1936, and today a handful of players have turned back to these remarkable instruments—some of them to play blues.

above > **Weissenborn didn't just make square-neck Hawaiian guitars—they also made some beautiful, delicate Spanish-necked steel-strings. This is a koa-wood Style C from 1925.**

right > **The multi-talented Ben Harper uses a variety of modern and vintage lap-style guitars.**

identifier

ben harper

Ben Harper, a 32-year-old Californian, is one of the finest "living blues" players in the US today—and he uses a 70-year old Weissenborn guitar. Although he crosses the boundaries from folk to rock, and has played with some of the biggest and most radical names in hip-hop, Harper is a true blues enthusiast, as familiar with the music of old-time greats like Charley Patton and Blind Willie McTell as with 1960s blues revivalists like Taj Mahal and Jimi Hendrix. Harper plays in several altered tunings, including DAFCGD. His treasured original Weissenborns include a Style 2, a Style 4, and a rare "teardrop"-shaped model. Keeping alive the traditional, Harper has commissioned both electric and acoustic Weissenborn-style guitars from modern makers such as Canopus, Bill Asher, and David Dart.

Herman Weissenborn's guitars were most popular in the 1920s.

koa wood—now an endangered timber—was a vital part of their unique sound.

decoration Weissenborn made a number of guitars with different levels of decorative "rope pattern" binding, from Style 1 to Style 4, costing between $40 and $79.

hollow necks Most models have necks that are actually hollow, thereby maximizing the internal volume. The scale lengths are generally around a medium 24.5 in.

the bridge saddle on a Weissenborn is straight, not angled, to give the best intonation with the slide held at 90 degrees to the strings.

labels Weissenborn also made guitars under the labels of Hilo, Kona, Shireson Lyric, and others.

other makers Other great flat-top Hawaiian-style koa instruments of the 1920s were made by Chris Knutsen, Oscar Schmidt, and Rudolph Dopyera, later of Dobro/National.

All-wood Hawaiian guitars fell from popularity in the latter years of the decade because of the overwhelmingly superior volume of the new resonator guitars.

the gibson style o a new concept

Orville Gibson was one of the greatest instrument designers in American history, and although after 1903 he had practically nothing to do with the company in Kalamazoo, Michigan that bore his name, his pioneering concepts still echo in the world of guitar making today.

Orville Gibson began making mandolins and guitars in the 1880s. He was a free thinker, abandoning many accepted rules for instrument construction and inventing many of his own. Primarily, it was Gibson who first dreamed up the concept of applying the carved top of the violin to the guitar and the mandolin. On an archtop guitar with a tailpiece, the force of the strings is transmitted directly downward against the arch; it's a far stronger design than that of the flat-top guitar with a fixed bridge, which has to endure twisting forces and inevitably suffers a far more limited lifespan. Orville's arched designs would flower some 25 years later, when designer Lloyd Loar joined Gibson in the 1920s and honed some of the finest instruments the company has ever produced, including the L-5 jazz guitar and the F-5 mandolin.

It was also Orville Gibson who introduced the concepts of oval soundholes in conjunction with bodies that were extremely large for their day, sometimes up to a massive 17.5 in. wide. Vitally, Gibson was one of the earliest to carry over the idea of steel strings from the mandolin to the guitar. Martin would not introduce a steel-string model until the 1920s.

Some of Orville's unique approaches to instrument design, however, have not stood the test of time. He believed that carving the necks and sides of his guitars from a single piece of wood would enhance the tone; time has proved him wrong. His archtop guitars were extremely heavily built, and though they were strong they had little of the volume or tone of conventionally strutted flat-top guitars from other makers. Yet many Gibson found their way into the hands of blues players like Big Bill Broonzy.

below > **Ahead of its time: this extra-wide Style O dates from 1908 and demonstrates many of the Gibson company's innovations, including an oval soundhole and a fixed bridge on an arched top.**

right > **Broonzy's later folk-blues sides were constantly re-released through the 1960s on albums like *Remembering Big Bill*.**

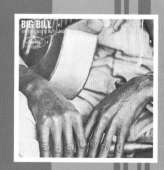

identifier

big bill broonzy

Around the time of William "Big Bill" Broonzy's first recording sessions in 1927 you'd have seen him holding a simple little Regal flat-top or a huge, showy Gibson Style O with a mandolin-style scroll (in the 1940s he played a blond Gibson L-7 archtop, in the 1950s a Martin OOO-28). Broonzy, born in 1893 in Scott, Mississippi, learned guitar after moving to Chicago in 1924, perfecting a lively, easygoing bare-finger style combining jazzy lead lines and driving bottom-string work. After taking the late Robert Johnson's place at a groundbreaking 1938 Carnegie Hall show, he soon became a well-loved entertainer. Broonzy's songwriting includes "Key To The Highway," "Just A Dream," "Get Back," "I Feel So Good," and several hundred others. An important figure in Chicago's growing small-band sound, playing on many rocking blues records and dabbling with electric guitar in 1947, Broozny then re-invented himself as an overalls-clad folk singer. He died in 1958, after sowing the seeds of the blues revival in Europe. Big Bill Broonzy never had the spooky mystery of Robert Johnson, nor the grit and fire of Muddy Waters, but his music was good-time all the way.

below > **Big Bill Broonzy holding a mandolin-scrolled Gibson Style O from the early 1920s.**

instruments As well as round-hole (L model) and oval-hole (O model) guitars, Gibson made mandolins, mandolas, mandocellos, and harp-guitars with either 12 or 18 strings.

"the gibson" logo first appeared on pegheads in 1905. Most Gibson guitars had wide, paddle-shaped headstocks with an inlaid moon and crescent motif and carved back that were flat across the center.

innovations such as carved tops and backs, internal tone bars, raised fingerboards, adjustable bridges, separate elevated pickguards, cutaway bodies to help higher-fret fingering, and adjustable truss-rods were pioneered by Gibson guitars of the early twentieth century.

style o started life in 1902 as a conventionally shaped oval-hole behemoth. By 1908 it had gained a mandolin-style scroll and a trapeze tailpiece and cost a whopping $150. The guitar was discontinued in 1923.

style l was the cheaper, much more common, round-hole, carved-top Style L guitars, with body shapes that would form the basis for Gibson's flat-top designs of the 1920s and 1930s. Models included the L-1 (1902–1926), L-2 (1902–1908 and 1924–1926) and the longer-surviving L-3 (1902–1933) and the larger, 16 in. wide round-hole L-4 (1912–1933).

right > **In Gibson terminology, "O" meant an oval soundhole while "L" meant a round soundhole. This black L model with special fingerboard inlays was probably custom-ordered in 1906. The body shape is identical to that of Robert Johnson's Gibson shown on page 71**

gibson I models   kalamazoo blues

Gibson made some spectacular instruments under the shadow of Orville Gibson. It took until 1924 for Gibson to put its name to a flat-top guitar. Around this time Gibson had adopted the services of the brilliant designer Lloyd Loar, and was busy refining the mandolin and the f-hole archtop guitar to a high level of near-perfection. In truth, Gibson considered flat-top guitars something of an inferior breed.

Nevertheless, they introduced a range of very decent flat-top guitars—the L-1, L-2, L-0, and L-00. St. Louis's Clifford "Grandpappy" Gibson played an L-1, as did Tennessee storytelling guitarist John Henry Barbee, while Robert Johnson's protégé Robert Lockwood Jr. chose a Gibson L-0. Gibson also introduced one of the finest little acoustics of all time in the shape of the Nick Lucas model, a real beauty made with high-quality woods, tasteful inlays, and an extra-deep, 4 ½ in. body for maximum richness and volume. Gibson might not have trumpeted the importance of these guitars at the time, but it does now. It's a sign of how these guitars have been re-evaluated that the company re-introduced various 1930s-style models as re-issues in the 1990s. Their current catalog includes the Blues King, a fingerpicking guitar based on the sunburst-top L-00.

gibson: the best blues guitars?

Gibson's flat-top guitars of the late 1920s and 1930s are now considered to be some of the best little country-style blues guitars ever built. Gibson's typical scale length of 24 ¾ in., shorter than a Martin's 25 ½ in., makes for easy handling, while the mahogany back and sides and the compact body design give a punchy, immediate sound with plenty of volume. By 1934 most Gibson flat-tops had been altered to offer 14 frets clear of the body, giving improved access to the 12th fret, but many players prefer the older 12-fret models.

above > **This classic mahogany and spruce Gibson L-00 dates from around 1934: earlier models, made since around 1930, were all black. Even today these guitars are known as some of the best recording tools around.**

scrapper blackwell

National and Gibson player Francis "Scrapper" Blackwell was born in Syracuse, North Carolina in 1903. He made his name as the guitar-playing partner of Leroy Carr, and the clarity of his jazzy, Lonnie Johnson-influenced style proved that the National was the only guitar capable of holding its own against a piano. Carr and Blackwell recorded many great numbers for Vocalion between 1928 and 1932, including the classic eight-bar blues "How Long, How Long." (Blackwell also penned "Kokomo Blues," which re-emerged through Robert Johnson as "Sweet Home Chicago.") Carr died in 1935, and a broken-hearted Blackwell retired from music. In 1959, after being coaxed into recording a new album, it seemed that Blackwell, at least, would finally get his dues. Tragic blues deaths, however, are not limited to the violent 1930s. In 1962 Scrapper Blackwell was shot in the back in an Indianapolis back alley. The murder was never solved.

identifier

prewar gibson flat-tops

gibson L-1—the model Robert Johnson is pictured with in one of two surviving photographs—was introduced in 1926. With a distinctive "rounded" 13 ½ in. wide body and a slightly arched top and back, it's considered a real blues classic. The L-1 gained a different bridge and a sunburst top by 1928, changed body shape to a squarer design in 1931, carried 14 frets clear of the body by 1932, a flat top and back around 1934 and was discontinued in 1937.

pricier L-2 started life in 1929, and alternated between rosewood and mahogany back and sides and 13 or 14 frets clear of the body.

gibson L-0, similar, but cheaper, was made of maple and spruce from 1926 until 1929, when it became an all-mahogany instrument. It changed to a 14 ¾ in. wide body in 1931, and was discontinued in 1933—save for a few examples from 1937.

1932 14-fret L-00 was cheaper still. It gained an imitation tortoiseshell pickguard in 1933 and a sunburst top in 1935, and survived until 1945.

1928–1938 nick lucas model is one of the most sought-after Gibson flat-tops of all, thanks to its extra-deep body. The L-C Century model was similar, and boasted an imitation pearl fingerboard.

left > **Scrapper Blackwell was the originator of "Kokomo Blues," later re-written by Robert Johnson as the famous "Sweet Home Chicago."**

robert johnson

king of the delta blues singers

Muddy Waters once saw Robert Johnson playing on the streets, and remembered that he was too scared to go near him. The mystical figure of Johnson had a powerful effect on all who heard him. Columbia's 1961 release of *Robert Johnson: King Of The Delta Blues Singers*—a shattering, world-tilting collection of songs—presented budding blues players with the new pinnacle of acoustic blues guitar. Johnson's vocals were high-pitched, eerie, sometimes seemingly scared to death, while his guitar playing combined driving rhythms, lightning turnarounds, groundbreaking boogie basslines, and stunning bottleneck work.

Robert Johnson was born in 1911 in Hazlehurst, Mississippi. As a teenage plantation worker, his harmonica playing drew derision from the older musicians. After marrying young he went traveling, and returned with a newfound prowess on the guitar. One of the blues' most enduring myths was that Johnson went to the crossroads and "sold his soul to the devil" in return for musical knowledge.

In truth, young Johnson must have studied hard: he learned most of all from an unrecorded blues guitarist called Ike Zinneman, he absorbed the work of Delta blues masters Charley Patton and Son House, and the style of Skip James's high-pitched "false" voice singing and unusual minor tuning playing. He also adored the early jazz/blues guitar master Lonnie Johnson, and drew elements from Scrapper Blackwell and Kokomo Arnold. Johnson knew exactly what he was doing, he learned his craft on street corners, in juke-joints, at dances, and from gramophone records. This bluesman perfected the three-minute blues format.

Johnson recorded his famous sides in hotel rooms in Dallas, Texas, between 1936 and 1937, turning his back to the recording engineer—not to hide his technique, as some have suggested, but possibly to exploit a sonic technique known as "corner loadin," playing his guitar straight at the wall to increase the immediacy and mid-range. Like all footloose blues players of the time, it's likely he went through a considerable number of guitars.

the complete artist

Johnson's untimely end in 1938 is as much a mystery as his recordings. Claims range from being poisoned by a jealous husband to death from syphilis; alternatively he may have died of pneumonia brought on by a combination of poisoning, liver damage, and moonshine.

Whatever the truth, all we're left with is the hair-raising power of songs like "Come On In My Kitchen" and "Hellhound On My Trail," which took the blues form to a whole new level. Robert Johnson was one of the finest and most complete blues artists of his generation, and arguably he's never been bettered. In the 1960s his songs were a central part of the acoustic blues repertoire: once Cream had recorded "Crossroads," and the Rolling Stones "Love In Vain," they also became part of the 1960s wave of blues rock. There's no fat on those 29 surviving sides, not a single unnecessary word or guitar figure. Every song is complete, miniature yet fully formed, honed to a terrifying edge.

left > **This clean, all-original Gibson L-1 dates from 1926, the year that a fixed bridge replaced the floating bridge and tailpiece**

right > **In one of two existing photographs. Robert Johnson is holding an already battered 1928 Gibson L-1. In another, he plays a cheaper Gibson-made Kalamazoo model**

sound of silver the national guitar

One of the most fascinating and charismatic instruments ever made, the National resonator guitar, first went into production 75 years ago. Its virtual death some 13 years later and its re-discovery during the 1960s folk-blues boom, and again in the 1980s, prompting the re-founding of the company, typifies the strange, circular path of the blues and the bewildering turbulence of guitar design in the twentieth century.

The 1920s guitar players, drowned out by every other instrument on the bandstand, so easily dispensed with, needed a super-loud guitar. In the mid 1920s a Hawaiian guitar player, George Beauchamp, approached two friends who ran a violin shop in Los Angeles, John and Rudy Dopyera, with an idea for a guitar which worked on the same principle as the Victrola gramophone. The Dopyera brothers approved: they'd likely already seen an English device called the Stroh violin, which passed the vibrations from the bridge to a small, sensitive circular disc and then on to an unwieldy gramophone horn. But they had a better idea: resonators built into the body of the guitar itself. After experimenting with many materials, John Dopyera hit on the perfect solution: aluminum.

below > **The original patent drawing for John Dopyera's tricone design, dated December 31st, 1929.**

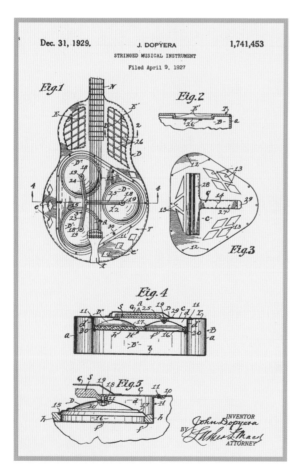

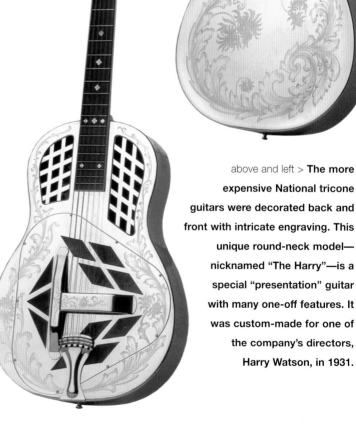

above and left > **The more expensive National tricone guitars were decorated back and front with intricate engraving. This unique round-neck model— nicknamed "The Harry"—is a special "presentation" guitar with many one-off features. It was custom-made for one of the company's directors, Harry Watson, in 1931.**

identifier

the tricone sound

National tricone guitars had bodies made of German silver, also known as white brass or nickel silver. An alloy of roughly around 65% copper, 20% zinc, and 15% nickel, it's the same material we use today for fretwire. The resonator system consisted of three 6 in. diameter cones, each one of almost pure aluminum, lathe-spun extremely thin—as little as 0.005 in.—and embossed with a radiating pattern of lines for the sake of added strength. The centers of the three cones were connected by a T-shaped bridge bar, which incorporated a maple insert which the strings rested directly upon. A triangular coverplate protected the delicate cones from nasty accidents.

National triplates have a distinctly different sound to the later, and cheaper, single-cone models: not as punchy and banjo-like, but sweet and rich, full of natural harmonics and a faint but unmistakable sense of natural reverb. Although a few blues players—Tampa Red, Black Ace, Memphis Minnie, and Peetie Wheatstraw—laid their hands on tricones, most of these expensive guitars went to jazz, calypso, and Hawaiian players, the company's preferred customers.

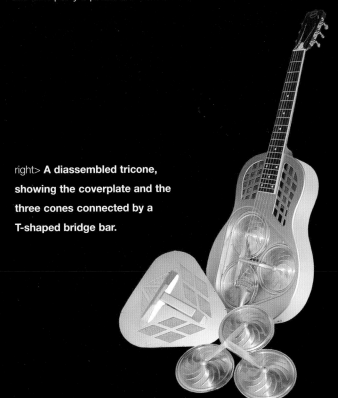

right> **A diassembled tricone, showing the coverplate and the three cones connected by a T-shaped bridge bar.**

national tricones

neck form was either square-neck, for playing lap-style, or round-neck, for playing conventionally, whether fingered or with a slide. All tricone necks met the body at the 12th fret.

round-neck models, also known as Spanish models, are rarer than square-necks. Wooden flat-top Hawaiian guitars like Gibsons and Martins have commonly been "converted" to round neck, but a National's metal construction makes the switch very difficult.

bodies were totally handmade by John and Rudy Dopyera with flat, not arched backs, "grilles" of woven strips of metal, and the cones sat on a wooden platform.

production-line tricones had cones that sat on metal platforms: they are considered the best-sounding of all.

tricone technology was also applied to mandolins, ukuleles, and tenor guitars. National's later single-cone mandolins are reputed to be the loudest stringed instruments ever built; Howard Armstrong of early string band the Mississippi Sheiks claimed that by hitting a chord he could kill a mosquito in mid-air.

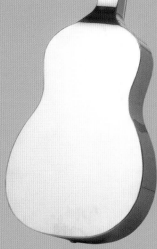
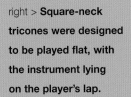

right > **Square-neck tricones were designed to be played flat, with the instrument lying on the player's lap.**

power of three **the national triplate guitar**

Under the brilliant organizational and manufacturing skills of John Dopyera the National triplate quickly took shape, and in 1926 the earliest all-handmade prototypes were ready. George Beauchamp took one of the first guitars to a party where Sol Hoopii, the leading Hawaiian-style player of the day, fell in love with the guitar. Beauchamp then proved his worth by persuading a rich cousin to invest $12,500 in a new production facility, and National guitars were on their way.

For any musician of the time, acquiring a National guitar meant a massive investment. The cheapest tricone, the very first triple-resonator Nationals, cost $125, the most expensive models $195. Nationals were unequivocally louder than any other guitar on the market, and for a few years, provided you could raise the cash, possessing one of these mechanically amplified guitars guaranteed that you'd be heard, seen, and remembered.

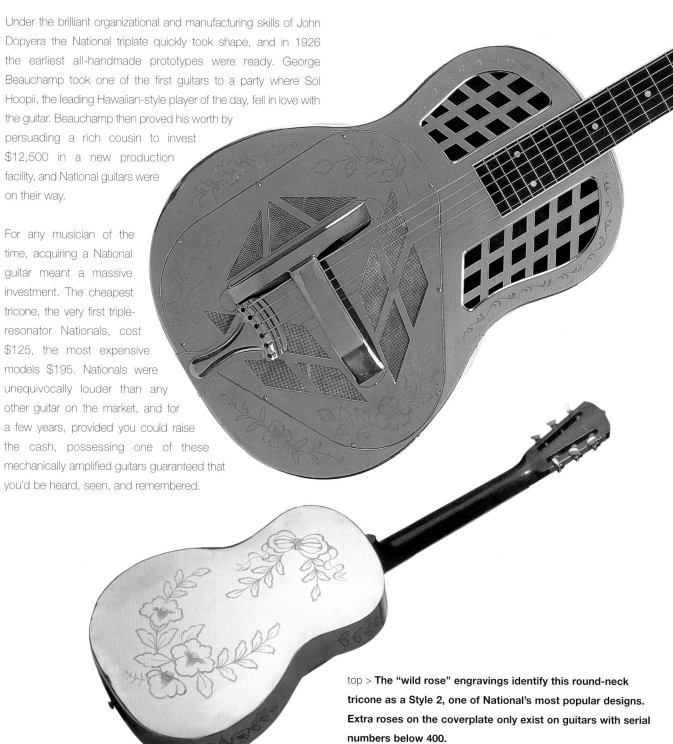

top > **The "wild rose" engravings identify this round-neck tricone as a Style 2, one of National's most popular designs. Extra roses on the coverplate only exist on guitars with serial numbers below 400.**

left > **A rear view of a round-neck Style 2 tricone.**

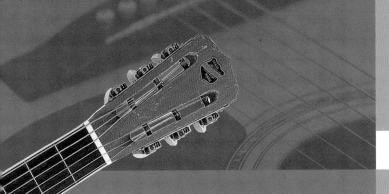

identifier

tampa red

The great Tampa Red, born in 1904 in Smithville, Georgia, was the first black musician to record with the fabulous new National guitar (he also played the kazoo, which can be a shock on first listen). Tampa Red wasn't named "the guitar wizard" for nothing; he had a great single-string slide technique featuring extraordinarily accurate string-damping and a full, fat sound. Though he recorded many sides with Georgia Tom Dorsey, and much of their material erred on the novelty side—the classic double entendre "It's Tight Like That" earned Tampa Red a then-fortune of $2,400—he could also deliver real Delta music, and composed great blues songs like "Black Angel Blues," "It Hurts Me Too," and "Love Her With A Feeling." Alongside his friend Big Bill Broonzy, Tampa Red ruled the Chicago scene in the 1930s and his home became a meeting place for all the blues musicians in town. Though in his later years Tampa Red turned to playing electric guitar, in his heyday he famously played a unique, show-stopping National tricone, a top-of-the-line, gold-plated Style 4. Tampa Red died in 1981, leaving the whereabouts of his priceless guitar unknown.

below > **Tampa Red, one of the acknowledged masters of the National guitar.**

styles

National made between 3,000 and 5,000 tricones in total but only 600 or 700 round-necks, which needed to be custom-ordered. All National guitars with German silver bodies came in four styles of decoration:

style 1 No body engraving save for a simple wavy line around the edge by the mid 1930s, pearl dot position markers, "National" decal on headstock, mahogany neck: cost: $125.

style 2 Engraved with a "wild rose" design on body and, on 1928–29 models, the coverplate too; pearl dot fret markers, "National" decal on headstock, mahogany neck: cost: $145.

style 3 Ornately engraved with one of five different "lily of the valley" designs, plus double-line borders, square pearl neck inlays, pearl "National" logo on ebony-fronted headstock: cost: $165.

style 4 The most elaborate of all, designed by Beauchamp himself, with one of two "chrysanthemum" patterns almost entirely covering the body, engraved pearloid headstock: cost: $195.

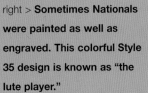

right > **Sometimes Nationals were painted as well as engraved. This colorful Style 35 design is known as "the lute player."**

palm trees and volcanos
the national style o

Tricone guitars were beautiful, and their sound could not be faulted: the prohibitive price, however, limited the number of players who could afford them. National needed to make a simpler, cheaper resonator instrument: a single-cone guitar.

At National, traditionalist John Dopyera fell out with rich playboy George Beauchamp, and in 1928 he left to form his own resonator guitar company, Dobro. Dopyera circumvented copyright problems—controversially, both the triple and the new single resonator system belonged to Beauchamp—by simply flipping the resonator around to become concave, and inventing a cast aluminum "spider" to transfer the vibrations of the bridge to the edge of the now-reversed cone.

Having differing cone systems, and Dopyera's choice of wooden bodies, these guitars have a distinctly different sound to Nationals. Dobros soon became the darlings of country and bluegrass players, while National's beautiful 12-fret Style O functioned as a Hawaiian guitar supreme, and also as the perfect blues guitar: unforgettably spectacular and terrifically loud.

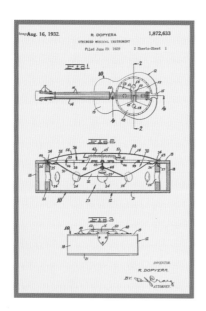

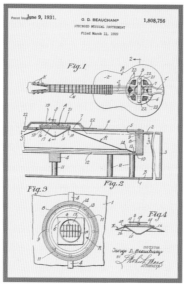

above > **Style O with coverplate removed, showing the spiral grooves on the speaker cone.**

left > **Rudy Dopyera patented the spider-bridged Dobro cone system (far left) just a few months after George Beauchamp claimed rights on the original biscuit-cone National design (right).**

right > **The great Son House, pictured in the 1960s. Without Son House's earlier influence there would have been no Robert Johnson and no Muddy Waters.**

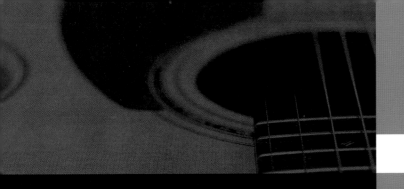

identifier

son house

The birth of Son House, in 1902, Riverton, Mississippi, provided the link between Charley Patton and the all-conquering Chicago blues of Muddy Waters, and gave us the most important Delta blues player of all. House, torn between the church and the blues all his life, was 25 before he first touched a guitar. It was after two years in prison for murder that he turned to performing full-time. Though no showman, House sang like a man possessed. "My Black Mama, Preachin' The Blues" and "Death Letter" are some of the deepest, most vital blues sides ever recorded. He played single-cone Nationals—a Style O, a Duolian or a Triolian, usually in open G tuning.

House was re-discovered in the 1960s (he had to re-learn his material from old records). His 1960s work is, uniquely, nearly as worthy of investigation as his 1930s Paramount sides and his 1941 Library of Congress recordings. He delivered performances with his powerhouse voice and driving, slashing guitar skills still intact. When he died in 1988, Son House left a vacancy for the title of Father of the Blues.

the style o

the "biscuit" The single 9 ½ in. resonator had a flat central platform which carried a 2 ft diameter maple "biscuit." The strings rested on a saddle which set into a slot on the biscuit.

early style O's had steel bodies, but soon they were made from bell-brass.

finish all Style O's had Hawaiian-style etchings on the front and back, which came in at least six variations, detailed in Bob Brozman's National Resonator Instruments (Centerstream Publishing 1993).

necks were maple, with a sunburst finish; the fingerboards were maple, dyed black.

1930 saw the debut of National's first single-cone guitar.
1930–1933 the f-holes were flat-cut.
1933–1941 f-holes with rolled edges.
1930–1935 The "National" logo on the headstock came with a plain decal.
1936–1937 with an arched decal.
1939–1940 over a celluloid facing.
1940–1941 with a metal logo over black.

top > **The ultimate blues guitar? This well-played early 1930s 12-fret Style O has the perfect combination of beauty, simplicity, and purpose.**
right > **the famous "Hawaiian" scene was literally sandblasted onto the body.**

plain power the national duolian

After the stock market crash of 1929, National's spectacular $60 Style O would eventually carry them through Depression-hit America, but they needed more sales. In 1931 they created the Duolian, a raw, basic single-resonator guitar with no trimmings whatsoever. National cut all the corners they could, abandoning the bell-brass body for a simple steel version. Steel accepts plating less readily than brass so the body was covered with a "frosted Duco" crystalline paint, which dried differently on every guitar, giving colors from gold to green to brown and black. National's new guitar cost $32.50, while the Sears catalog sold an unbranded version for a paltry $29. This plain, but value-packed Duolian became the chosen tool of hundreds of blues guitarists in the 1930s, including Blind Gary Davis, Bukka White, Blind Boy Fuller, Son House, Bo Carter of the Mississippi Sheiks, and many others.

Single-cone Nationals are even louder than tricones, with a punchier, more strident quality. The tone wasn't as sweet as the tricone and the sustain considerably shorter, but for pure attack and banjo-like penetration a $30 Duolian, when strung with the super-heavy strings of the time, 0.013 in. or more in the treble, and struck with a thumbpick and two finger-picks, could out-punch a $200 Style 4 tricone every time.

below left and right > **The base-model National Duolian was the company's biggest seller during the Depression, and before the advent of electricity it was the loudest guitar that $30 could buy.**

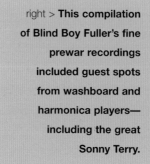

right > **Top fingerpicker Blind Boy Fuller, here playing a National Duolian with a capo at the first fret.**

right > **This compilation of Blind Boy Fuller's fine prewar recordings included guest spots from washboard and harmonica players— including the great Sonny Terry.**

Classic Jazz masters

Country Blues
Blind Boy Fuller
1935-1940

identifier

blind boy fuller

Ace fingerpicker and prime exponent of the light, cheerful East Coast Piedmont style of guitar playing shared by Gary Davis and Blind Blake, Fulton "Blind Boy Fuller" Allen was born in 1908 in Wadesboro, North Carolina. His gradual and complete loss of sight by the age of 20 gave him little choice but to play on the streets for a living. Fuller moved to the tobacco town of Winston-Salem and later to Durham, where he would play for the workers as they left the factory. He could perform blues, naughty novelty songs, ragtime and slide blues styles with equal aplomb, and though he enjoyed only a short recording spell (1935–1940), he recorded nearly 150 songs. He would surely have gone on to greater things had he not died of a kidney ailment in 1941, but still, Blind Boy Fuller was the last big success story of all the prewar country blues guitarists.

duolian figures

sales National made in excess of 1,500 Duolians each year during the 1930s. In all, they sold around 10,000 Duolians and Triolians.

body shape The 12-fret body shape with flat-cut f-holes changed to a 14-fret design with rolled-edge f-holes in 1935.

necks changed from maple or mahogany to basswood in 1936.

serial numbers Duolians, like other Nationals, carry their serial numbers stamped on the end of the headstock and dating guitars from these numbers is difficult.

1927–1935 National used a different number series for each style of instrument.

1931–1936 Duolians came with both "C" prefix and "O" prefix numbers.

1935–1936 with "E" prefix or no-prefix numbers.

1931–1932 guitars made for Sears, Roebuck come with "R" prefix serial numbers.

1936–1941 they standardized the system, but changed it every year.

top right > **Changing strings might take a little longer... but there's nothing so elegant as a slotted headstock.**
above > **Many National serial numbers were stamped onto the top of the headstock.**

hawaiian dreams
the 14-fret national style o

In a big shift in design philosophy in 1934, National adopted the 14-fret neck pioneered by C. F. Martin in 1929 on the OM flat-top guitar. Today many National lovers consider the original 12-fret models more beautiful, but the new guitar's shorter body and longer, easier-playing neck certainly helped National to keep up with the times. Other features changed too: slotted headstocks were abandoned, and replaced with a solid, more production-friendly design; the f-holes lost their dangerously sharp knife-edges; and the coverplates changed from a drilled "colander" style to diamond-shaped slots now affectionately known as "chicken feet." As always, however, the bodies were made of bell-brass, nickel-plated, and then lightly sandblasted through a rubberized template.

There's a great deal of inconsistency in the sound of vintage Nationals: sometimes corners were cut in the fast-running factory. The hand-spun cones varied wildly in thickness. Each individual body was stressed and strengthened by banging in dowels (from a couple, to as many as seven) between the front of the body and the back. Nobody to this day knows exactly why one National sounds so smooth while another, perhaps made the same day, sounds so harsh.

below left and right > **This fine mid 1930s Style O has the new-design body, allowing a longer neck with better access to the upper frets. The headstock, however, is the old "slotted" type.**

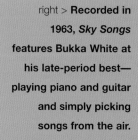

right > **Recorded in 1963, *Sky Songs* features Bukka White at his late-period best— playing piano and guitar and simply picking songs from the air.**

bukka white

Booker T. Washington White, known as "Bukka" ever since his name was misspelled on a record label, was born in 1906 in Houston, Mississippi, a cousin to B. B. King. He was a power-house performer, with a uniquely percussive slide style played in open G tuning on a steel-bodied National—usually a Duolian or a Triolian.

In and out of prison in the 1930s, White made his best recordings in 1940, including "Shake 'Em On Down" and "Fixin' To Die." His remarkable lyrics are a window onto the real blues life—riding the rails, working on Parchman Farm—and his compelling, rhythmic guitar style earned him a reputation of a break-down artist: People would dance so hard, they literally broke the floorboards. Bukka White was re-discovered by white blues guitarist John Fahey in 1963 and played many great concerts before his death in 1977.

below > **Good times guaranteed: The compelling Bukka White.**

identifier

other national guitars

style n the rare early 1930s single-cone Style N National looked like a plainer Style O, but the body was made from expensive German silver.

don From 1934 to 1936 the company dropped the Style N and replaced it with the spectacular Don model, the fanciest single-cone National, with three types of engraving and a pearloid-faced headstock.

wooden bodies In the late 1930s National started fitting resonators to wooden bodies bought in from Kay, Harmony, and even Gibson.

collegians made in the late 1930s, were the cheapest Nationals ever, finished in yellow paint and with simple concentric punched holes on the coverplates.

el trovador was the best-quality wooden National, with Kay-manufactured 12-fret mahogany-veneered bodies and a sound comparable to the metal models.

trojan, estralita, and rosita guitars, muddy-toned and less desirable, with laminated birch or basswood bodies supplied by Harmony.

aragons were the largest Nationals of all, wood-bodied, a full 18 in. wide, with a thin top designed to improve the sound—among the loudest Nationals of all.

above > **A pearloid headstock overlay identifies this as a Don, National's finest-quality single-cone guitar.**

from wood to steel
the national triolian

The National Triolian, chosen guitar of Scrapper Blackwell, the young Sister Rosetta Tharpe, guitar/harmonica player Hammie Nixon, and even, in one photograph, of Duke Ellington, has a complex history. Originally National planned a wooden-body tricone guitar, making around a dozen prototypes. By the time the guitar hit production in 1928, however, the Triolian had become a wooden-bodied, single-cone model, finished in "Polychrome" paint—a highly unusual yellow with red and blue highlights—and decorated with floral decal patterns. These guitars sound very similar to metal-bodied Nationals, but with a slightly warmer bass.

By 1929, after another change of mind, the Triolian gained a steel body, and by 1930 the model appeared with two different finishes: a green-tinted Polychrome and a yellow to brown "walnut" sunburst. In the last years of National, from 1937 to 1941, the guitar came painted to simulate rosewood.

The Triolian was a big seller for National. At $45 it offered a good deal more glamor than the bargain-basement Duolian, and it was certainly a loud guitar, though the steel-bodied ones can sound slightly harsh. Many blues players appreciated having a steel guitar, though: for protection should someone invade the stage to begin a "discussion" about an errant girlfriend. There's also the true story of a steel guitar with a bullet hole in the front—but just a bump in the back. A National could save your life.

left top and bottom > **This Polychrome Triolian, serial number 1517, is one of the original wooden-bodied single-cone 1929 production models.**

right > **Four wooden-bodied Nationals. From the top, a Rosita model with a "fiddle" coverplate; a Kay-bodied El Trovador; a round-neck Havana with a "violin" finish; and a natural square-neck Havana.**

parts bin specials

The old idea that Nationals are metal and Dobros are wood is not borne out by the facts. Dobro did indeed make metal-bodied guitars, and National made a huge number of affordable wood-bodied instruments in the 1930s by the simple method of buying in bodies from other, established makers and adding their own patented hardware.

On many models—including the Rosita, Trojan, and Estrellita—the woodwork was carried out by Harmony in Chicago. Harmony-bodied Nationals are of lesser quality than the National-made wooden-bodied Triolian. Harmony also supplied some bodies for the ungainly—but extremely loud—Aragon, National's largest-ever guitar.

Another Chicago instrument-making giant, Kay, was the source of bodies for the Havana and the El Trovador. The Havana cost $50, more than the metal-bodied Duolian, but few were sold thanks perhaps to the slightly clumpy shape and the ill-placed f-holes. The pick of the bunch was the El Trovador, which was constructed of thick, high-quality laminated mahogany. It had a subtle, delicate body outline with elongated upper bouts, and the coverplate was exactly the same as the ones found on a Style O or Triolian. Some players feel the El Trovador sounds just as good as a metal-bodied National.

identifier

triolian timeline

1928 Twelve prototype wooden-bodied tricones are made.

1929 The first production Triolians are wooden-bodied, single-cone models with a number of decal motifs, including anemones, Hawaiian hula girls, and stenciled palm trees.

1930 Wooden body changes to steel. A large batch of Bakelite-neck models proved to be unstable, and half were re-necked.

1930–1934 Painted Polychrome finish includes pale green and brown sunburst with a black stenciled Hawaiian scene.

1935 Design changed from 12 frets clear of the body to 14.

1936 Slotted headstock changed to solid.

1937 Fake rosewood painted finish with added celluloid pickguard.

1941 Triolian discontinued.

top right > **A Triolian headstock: National decals came in various colors, including black and green backgrounds with "Triolian" in black or red.**
right > **One of the last Triolians from the late 1930s with an all-over simulated rosewood finish.**

electric archtop guitars
a national first

National resonator guitars slipped into a gap in time between the acoustic guitar and the development of a practical electric model. By the mid 1930s, pickup and amplifier technology was such that it suddenly became feasible to buy a pickup as an accessory, mount it on your regular guitar, purchase an amplifier, and step into a brand new world of amazing audibility.

Though the resonator guitar was manufactured until the 1940s—after all, electricity had yet to reach many remote areas—for the next decade or more, the new blues guitar became a regular archtop jazz model, modified to accept a simple single-coil pickup.

The adoption of this new style of guitar brought a change in the whole style of blues guitar playing itself. The amplified guitar suddenly allowed players to integrate themselves, switching from solo, or at most small duos or trios, into larger groups. The playing style changed to fit, with more widespread standard tuning and musicians at last able to play jazz-based chordal accompaniment and saxophone-influenced single-note lines with equal facility. City-based players like Tampa Red knew that even with the relatively low-powered amplifiers of the day, the new breed of electric guitars was the key to getting many more gigs in larger, noisier bars and clubs. By now, vocalists were often singing through microphones into rudimentary public address systems. Horns and pianos could keep up—and now so too could the guitar. Pickups and amps were expensive, but a working guitarist often found that they paid for themselves in no time at all.

above > **This wonderful old National archtop has a blade-type factory pickup not dissimilar to Gibson's "Charlie Christian" pickup. The matching National amplifier dates from the same period.**

right > **Early Chicago bluesman Tampa Red was one of the best-known slide guitarists of the 1920s and 1930s. Here he's playing without a slide—but still with a thumbpick—on a 1940s electric National archtop.**

identifier

memphis minnie

The blues was no men-only club. Singers like the great Bessie Smith had been among the biggest blues stars of the 1920s, but when it came to guitar playing Memphis Minnie was the real deal, once beating both Tampa Red and Big Bill Broonzy in a picking contest. Born Lizzie Douglas in 1897 in Algiers, Louisiana, at age 13 Minnie moved to Memphis and soon became an accomplished street performer. She first recorded in 1929 and sustained her success across an incredible four decades, hopping from label to label and, with certain good judgment, from one influential guitar-playing husband to another. Her best guitar work is mostly found between her first recordings and the period 1938 to 1942, at which point she became one of the first blues artists to play the electric guitar. Though Memphis Minnie also played a Stella and a National tricone, in her heyday she was most often pictured with a 1940s National archtop guitar with an added pickup.

below > **Memphis Minnie, one of the great women blues guitarists, pictured with her 1940s National archtop guitar.**

national electrics

sold By the time Memphis Minnie's famous electric archtop was made, the National name had been sold and the guitars were being made by a different, far larger concern in Chicago.

the first electric guitars were being developed by the original Californian National facility before the changeover.

early electric guitars/mandolins were made by National by 1934, in response to the coming of the electric age and the inevitable demise of the resonator guitar.

the "reso-lectric" was National's attempt, around 1939, to market a pickup system for their resonator guitars. The system consisted of a pickup, ready-mounted in a large circular plastic plate. Existing National owners could unscrew their coverplates, remove the resonator, mount the new unit, and plug their guitars into an amplifier (unfortunately, they would lose all semblance of acoustic volume). The company also sold these instruments under the name of National Silvo guitars direct from the factory.

right > **From acoustic to electric—this square-neck 12-fret Style O was sent back to the factory in the late 1930s to have its resonator, coverplate, and tailpiece removed and replaced with National's new drop-in pickup system.**

the resonator revival
re-founding national

The 1980's appearance of the National guitar on the sleeve of Dire Straits' *Brothers In Arms*—a priceless piece of publicity—led indirectly to the re-founding of the National guitar company. Dire Straits' Mark Knopfler, a long-time resonator guitar fan, saw Muddy Waters and Son House in the late 1960s. Knopfler reveals, he "started seeking out any artist associated with the National: Bukka White, Blind Boy Fuller. I bought my first one, a 1928 Style 2 rose-pattern tricone, from an old couple for $120—I was only making $15 a week! It's a real guitar-players' guitar...those tricones can really play."

below > **The use of a 1936 National Style O by Mark Knopfler helped push these unique guitars back into the spotlight.**

"The one on the album, though, is a 1936 14-fret Style O. It's a magical guitar. I can't explain it. I love the etching on the back, the palm tree, the volcano, the lovers in the canoe—it's like an old movie, cheesy but cool. In the pre-electric days, Nationals must have been a godsend for street-singers...since you can't bend the strings you have to think of other things to do, so the beauty actually comes from the guitar's limitations."

"If I could go back in time to see original country blues being played, I'd choose Blind Willie McTell and Blind Willie Johnson. To be in the same room as those guys...wonderful. It's fascinating to listen to modern rap, as well—in a way, it comes from the very same place."

identifier

john hammond

A leading exponent of rough, real blues and the National guitar for over 30 years, John Hammond arrived in New York in the early 1960s in time to meet and play with his heroes: Bukka White, Furry Lewis, John Hurt, Skip James, Big Joe Williams and many more. He discovered his first 1930s Duolian sitting in a guitar store. "It was incredibly hard to play," Hammond laughs. "They're so loud that if you make one tiny mistake, it's like, 'Aaaargh!'...I ended up playing professionally for four or five years before I had the nerve to play the National on stage. My main one these days is a Duolian with a maple neck. No matter how badly I treat it, no matter how rusty it seems to get, it still looks and sounds great."

above > **John Hammond has stayed true to his Nationals for nearly 40 years. At one period in the 1960s, in New York, he had both Jimi Hendrix and Eric Clapton in his backing band.**

resonator guitars today

1989 The modern National company, headed by Don Young and McGregor Gaines, made their first guitars, and for the first three years, until they could afford metal stamping dies, all their guitars were wooden-bodied.

models Today National make dozens of different models, including tricones and single resonators (in both biscuit-cone and Dobro-style spider-cone formats), with square or round necks.

style o Hawaiian-etched, is National's best modern seller. It's also available in unetched N and 12-string versions.

the delphi is National's modern baked-finish, steel-bodied equivalent to the Duolian.

tricones come in painted Polychrome, Styles 1, 1.5, 2, 3 and 4, plus the 97 with colored etching.

new designs include a long-scale tricone baritone guitar, the cutaway-body Radio-Tone Bendaway, a resonator bass guitar and the influential Reso-Lectric—a classic modern blues instrument combining a solid body with a magnetic pickup and a piezo-fitted resonator.

top > **The present-day 12-fret National Style 2 is a fancier version of the nickel-plated 1930s Style O, complete with sandblasted Hawaiian scenes.**
above > **The fine-sounding National Delphi recreates the bare-bones appeal of the 70-year old Duolian design.**

future blues the resonator guitar now

By the 1990s, a whole new resonator guitar movement had emerged. Nationals gave some players the old-time vibe they needed: others took the instrument in a new direction. Rock/blues artists have long turned to Nationals: Stevie Ray Vaughan, for instance, recorded with a Duolian that reputedly belonged to Blind Boy Fuller.

The late Rainer Ptacek of Tucson, Arizona coined an innovative new blues style by combining the sounds of vintage resonator guitars—a 1930s National and a 1930s wood-bodied Dobro—with high-tech, pedal-operated digital looping. Chris Whitley makes records by manipulating the sounds of various Nationals, including a Duolian, a Triolian, and a brass-bodied Style O with the latest computer editing techniques. Keb' Mo' carries forward the legacy of Robert Johnson and Tampa Red on a collection of guitars including an original National Style O, a modern National Reso-Phonic electro-resonator guitar and a high-quality modern resonator by Beltona. The UK's Michael Messer also plays Beltona guitars, plus various vintage originals including a unique 1937 12-string National; contemporary roots player Steve James plays a modern National Reso-Phonic Style N guitar; Corey Harris combines blues, jazz, and African influences in a new and exciting way; and National expert, collector, and player Bob Brozman introduces audiences worldwide to the full range of resonator guitar music—not just blues, but old-time, calypso, and Hawaiian styles too.

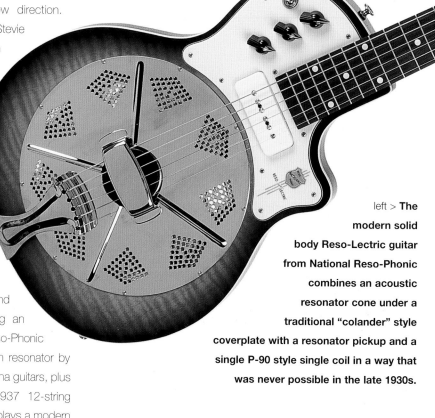

left > **The modern solid body Reso-Lectric guitar from National Reso-Phonic combines an acoustic resonator cone under a traditional "colander" style coverplate with a resonator pickup and a single P-90 style single coil in a way that was never possible in the late 1930s.**

right > **Chris Whitley mixes old-school sounds with up-to-the-minute technology. He plays both fretting and slide styles, with a homemade bottleneck sawn from a bicycle handlebar. Here he's playing a vintage National Duolian.**

far right > **Kevin Moore, a.k.a. Keb' Mo', carries on the blues tradition playing bare-fingered on his original National Style O.**

the electro-resonator guitar: sound secrets

Amplifying resonator guitars has always been a problem. A microphone, the traditional solution, requires the player to be constantly aware of the guitar's exact positioning. Adding a simple magnetic electric guitar pickup provides plenty of stage volume, but much of the tonal character of the resonator itself will be lost.

Recently, new developments—piezo transducers that amplify metal cones, and electronics capable of mixing and blending the outputs of two different pickups—have given rise to a whole new style of blues guitar. National's Reso-Electric model, for instance, combines the convenience of a small solid-bodied guitar with 70-year-old resonator technology, allowing the player to choose any point on a line between a reasonable amplified "traditional" resonator sound and the high volume and long sustain of a solid body electric guitar.

identifier

the resonator explosion

All over the world, a number of guitar companies now specialize in resonator guitars.

dobro now revived, are now making good-quality resonators such as the 14-fret, single cone Steel 90.

fine resophonic guitars a Paris-based company, make a whole range of highly-regarded wooden and metal-bodied, single-cone and electro-resonator models.

f1 resonator instruments in the UK have experimented with combining low-tech cone technology with modern guitar-building materials such as carbon fiber.

tim scheerhorn based in Kentwood, Michigan, makes mainly lap-style Dobros but also produces Spanish-style National-type guitars.

beltona resophonic guitars of New Zealand make a whole range of cone-driven guitars, including single-cones, tricones, and electro-resonators.

in the far east a wide range of single-cone resonator guitars are manufactured. The sound varies, but most can be improved by the addition of a quality replacement cone.

amistar a Czech company, led the way with an affordable reproduction of the round-neck National Tricone guitar. Other companies such as Continental use the Amistar body.

left > **Britain's Michael Messer, one of the very best of the new breed of resonator players, blends styles old and new.**

the electric age a new dawn

The identity of the first electric blues guitarist is unknown. It could be that someone got hold of Adolph Rickenbacker's "electric frying pan"—a six-stringed solid guitar of rudimentary design with a "horseshoe" pickup that ran around, not under the strings—soon after its introduction in 1932. Blues players certainly would have known about National's first electrics of the middle 1930s. The development of the electric guitar was held back not by speaker technology, nor pickup technology; the problem lay in between, with the amplifier.

Around 1928, and the arrival of crude public address systems, companies fought to produce the first reliable, portable instrument amplifiers. In 1929, Stromberg-Voisinet advertised an amp for $165, but their pickup—simple soundboard-amplifying piezos—hardly sounded impressive. Then, in 1932, the Electro amp arrived. Manufactured by Ro-Pat-In of Los Angeles, the Electro partnered a proper Spanish guitar with a magnetic pickup designed by ex-National man George Beauchamp. Others soon followed: Rickenbacker, Vivi-Tone, Audio-Vox, and Vega all had semi-professional electric instrument/amp sets on the market by 1933 (frighteningly, the Volu-Tone amp of the same year required the pickup to be charged with a burst of lethal high-voltage current). Dobro stepped into the electric market in 1934, and Gibson finally broke cover in 1935.

the gibson es-150

In 1935 Gibson debuted the EH-150 electric Hawaiian guitar and the EM-150 mandolin, and raced their first-ever proper production electric Spanish guitar to the market in 1936, a year after National. A young player from Oklahoma City, Charlie Christian, emerged to take advantage of the new guitar's sound and response, and soon found a job with the Benny Goodman quintet. Christian's vibrant, swinging amplified lines not only established the guitar as a jazz solo voice equal to the saxophone or trumpet: it also had a seismic effect on a new generation of blues players, including T-Bone Walker. The electric archtop guitar heralded the dawn of a fresh blues guitar style, heavily jazz-influenced and combining punchy, hornlike chords with thrilling single- and double-string soloing.

identifier

gibson's prewar electrics

1936 Gibson's first real electric guitar, the 16 ¼ in. wide ES-150, had a large, extremely heavy "bar" pickup unit with three adjustment screws visible between pickup and bridge. Blues guitarist Homesick James was playing one by around 1938.

1938 The cheaper, 14 ¼ in. wide ES-100 was introduced. It carried the same pickup, but with a plainer cream-colored plastic pickup surround.

1938-1940 The ES-250—probably the finest prewar electric guitar of all—was a deluxe version of the ES-150, with a blond finish and an improved bar pickup, now known as the "Charlie Christian" pickup. Houston pianist/blues singer Amos Milburn, also a guitarist, played one.

1940 Gibson made the ES-300, a 17 in. wide archtop jazz guitar with a huge 6 in. long pickup mounted slantwise across the strings. After just a few months, the pickup was discarded in favor of a smaller model.

world war two Gibson ceased production of all their electric instruments with the onset of World War Two.

right > **Gibson's ES-300 of 1940 with the extraordinary—but thankfully short-lived—"long" pickup, an attempt to make the bass strings as warm and the treble strings as sharp-sounding as possible.**

left > **The astonishing Charlie Christian, one of the first-ever musicians to record with an electric guitar, playing thumb-style on his Gibson ES-150.**

gibson after the war
embracing electric guitars

After the war, America's major guitar makers embraced the electric guitar, though Martin carried on making fine acoustic flat-tops just as before. Gibson, however, swiftly refined its electric line with re-designed pickups, larger bodies, and plenty of emphasis on affordability. Gretsch and Epiphone, Gibson's main rivals in the prewar archtop jazz market, followed suit. National/Valco was soon producing thousands of cheap yet cheerful hollow-bodied electrics.

Amplifiers changed fast, too: 1930s combos had small speakers, often no tone controls, and an output that rarely exceeded 10 or 15 watts, but by the late 1940s musicians could buy flamed-maple bandstand behemoths like the huge Epiphone Electar Zephyr. For the whole of the 1940s, however, the actual design of electric guitars seemed to be stuck in a time warp. Despite the prewar success of solid body Hawaiian guitars, no maker was prepared to risk their reputation on a solid body electric Spanish guitar. They were convinced that musicians would only accept fully acoustic guitars with added pickups.

gibson es-125:
all the blues you need

The P-90 pickup and a light, almost acoustic archtop construction is a soulful, if hard to handle combination. In the late 1940s the young B. B. King owned an ES-125, a basic noncutaway Gibson archtop with a single P-90 pickup. From the 1970s onward, Delaware-born slide bluesman George Thorogood choose a later, thin-bodied, twin-pickup version of the same guitar to remind concert-going crowds just why Robert Johnson, John Lee Hooker, and Elmore James still mean so much.

left > **Full-throttle blues rocker George Thorogood in the 1980s with his thinline twin-pickup ES-125TD.**

right > **"The Peptikon Boy"— a young B. B. King with a Gibson ES-125D advertising a popular medicine on radio WDIA, Memphis, 1949.**

identifier

the p-90 pickup

After the war Gibson abandoned the bulky "Charlie Christian" pickup and worked on a compact new unit to fit a variety of new models. The P-90 was a single-coil unit designed to be fitted into, not on top of, the face of the guitar. Clamped in place by just two screws, one at each end of black plastic pick-up casing, it was impossible to raise or lower it toward or away from the strings. However, Gibson eventually offered some semblance of control over string balance by making the six polepieces individually height-adjustable. P-90-equipped guitars came with both a volume and a tone control, and became Gibson's signature electric tone for the next ten years.

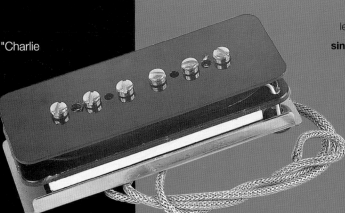

left > **The fat-sounding single-coil P-90 was the mainstay of Gibson's electric range before the advent of the humbucker in 1957.**

gibson electrics of the 1940s

es-125 Gibson's full-sized entry-level electric-acoustic guitar of 1946. Now 16 ¼ in. wide, the ES-125 carried a single nonadjustable P-90 in the neck position and adjustable polepieces. It would remain unaltered in Gibson's catalog until 1970.

prewar es-150 remodeled, with a full 17 in. body to carry the new P-90 pickup, it gained "trapezoid" fingerboard markers in 1950 and lasted until 1956.

1946 es-300 added multiple body and fingerboard binding. Initially with one P-90, it gained two P-90s in 1948 and was discontinued in 1952.

es-350 of 1947 was the premier electric model, with a rounded body cutaway for easy upper neck access. It gained a second P-90 in 1948 and added a second tone control in 1952.

es-140 was a small-bodied, three-quarter-scale budget model.

gibson's es-175 of 1949, the great jazz workhorse, boasted a sharp body cutaway. The first single-P-90 model lasted right up to 1971, with a twin-pickup model introduced in 1953.

the gibson es-5 triple treat

In 1949, with the success of guitars like the affordable ES-125 already confirmed, Gibson regained its unrivalled prewar reputation for making top-line jazz guitars with the introduction of a fabulous new electric instrument. This was the ES-5— "ES" to indicate Electric Spanish, "5" to recall the groundbreaking L-5 archtop of the 1920s. The ES-5 was masterminded by Ted McCarty, the new Gibson boss who would go on to oversee the company's greatest electric guitars, including the Les Paul, the Flying V, and the ES-335.

The new ES-5 cleverly covered all the possibilities. It was built to please the traditionalists and incorporated the highest standards of fine archtop construction, including laminated figured maple back, sides, top, and neck, and gold hardware. It also came equipped with a startling array of three P-90 pickups, all linked to a control system that offered individual volumes for each pickup, together with a master tone control. The appearance of an instrument of this quality from a company as careful of its reputation as Gibson showed that the electric guitar was here to stay.

The guitar rapidly built up a significant following, especially among blues players: many of the greats—including B. B. King, T-Bone Walker, and later Eric Clapton—fell for the ES-5's combination of rich looks and super-warm sound.

top right > **Gibson's expensive flamed-maple ES-5 was the first three-pickup guitar on the market. This natural-finish 1957 model has an added Bigsby vibrato; it's the later "Switchmaster" version, with a four-way selector on the upper treble bout.**

right > **The Epiphone Zephyr Blues Deluxe offers a modern facsimile of the jazzy jump blues guitar sound.**

right > **T-Bone Walker's jazzy, extrovert guitar lines form the link between Charlie Christian and B. B. King.**

t-bone walker

The whole of modern electric blues lead guitar is traceable back to Aaron Thibeaux "T-Bone" Walker, born in 1910, in Linden, Texas. Clad in a sharp suit, and with his blond Gibson ES-5 held at almost 90 degrees to his body, Walker played funky, swinging blues with immaculate style and taste. Jazz guitarists Charlie Christian, Eddie Lang, Lonnie Johnson, and Eddie Durham had pioneered horn-style electric guitar lines: by 1940 Walker had moved to LA, and there he combined these new moves with the blues he'd learned at the feet of Blind Lemon Jefferson in the 1920s.

In T-Bone's blues you can hear jazzy sliding ninth and sixth chords, early echoes of B. B. King's single-note style, and double-stopped ⅚ riffs that prefigure the intros to Chuck Berry's 1950's pop/blues crossover hits. Famous for his choreographic routine of splits, jumps, and playing behind his head, T-Bone was also a great songwriter, bandleader, and arranger, responsible for all-time classics like "They Call It Stormy Monday," "T-Bone Shuffle," and "West Side Baby." T-Bone Walker recorded from 1929 through to 1970 and died in 1975. In his golden period—between 1942 and 1957, particulary around 1947—you can hear urban contemporary blues being created before your ears.

identifier

timeline

1949 The 17-in.-wide, rounded cutaway, all-maple ES-5 debuted.

Gibson adorned the package with all its top-line trimmings, including multiple bindings, pearl block fingerboard markers, and gold hardware.

Three P-90 pick-ups were connected to three volume controls and a master tone control.

mid 1950s The ES-5 was also offered with the new Tune-O-Matic adjustable bridge and Alnico V single-coil pickups.

1955 The factory fitted the guitar with extra controls: a separate volume and tone for each pickup, plus a four-position sliding pickup selector, and re-named the guitar the ES-5 Switchmaster.

1956 The Switchmaster gained a new tubular tailpiece, humbucking pickups in 1958, and a pointed cutaway in 1960. It was discontinued in 1962.

above > **A guitarist named Jimmy Pruett ordered this fine sunburst model in 1957, the last year of the single-coil P-90 pickups, and added his name to the pickguard. The "Switchmaster" selector offered all three pickups individually, or all three together.**

the fender bass changing music forever

Up until now, the traditional double bass had never been a big part of blues. Unwieldy and almost impossible to amplify effectively in the days of vocals-only PA systems, basses did appear alongside saxophones in urban jump blues bands of the 1940s, but most electric guitarists worth their salt could provide pumping bass lines when needed. Many hot combos, like Sonny Boy Williamson's legendary King Biscuit Time radio band, simply employed drums, guitar, and amplified harp.

All that changed when Leo Fender's Precision Bass arrived on the scene in 1951. Unlike early attempts at electric basses by Gibson's Lloyd Loar, Ampeg's Everett Hull and Rickenbacker—all upright instruments with questionable pickups—the Fender bass was a tough solid-body guitar with an easy-to-handle 34-in. scale length and guitar-style frets that meant it played in tune. Through one of Fender's own amplifiers, bassists could at last be heard and were free to move around the stage. Guitarists, meanwhile, found themselves liberated from holding down the bottom, and could concentrate on rhythm and lead playing without leaving gaping holes in the sound. The Fender bass has had more of an effect on popular music than almost any other instrument of the twentieth century.

below > **The original and best: Leo Fender's portable, great-sounding Precision of 1951 was the first-ever electric bass guitar. Early examples followed the Telecaster in design with a flat slab body, a black Bakelite scratchplate, and the controls mounted on a metal plate.**

right > **Fender's 1953 flyer for the Precision and the original 15-in. speaker Bassman combo promised "a new sensation for bass players" that made "previously fast, difficult passages easy to play." Unlike most guitar sales literature, this was an understatement.**

identifier

the blues goes bass

Jazz bassists might have sneered at Fender's weird-looking four-stringed guitar, but blues artists knew a good thing when they saw one. B. B. King was one of the first bandleaders to order a Fender bass, probably as early as 1953. Down in New Orleans, guitar showman extraordinaire Guitar Slim knew he had to get a Fender bass in his band just to keep up, and soon persuaded his bassist Lloyd Lambert to buy one. In St Louis Ike Turner's Kings of Rhythm were not to be outdone, and brought the power and convenience of Leo Fender's invention on board as soon as they could. In Chicago, Muddy Waters' bassist Dave Myers turned the city on to the new sound. By the middle of the 1950s a fair number of the top-earning blues and R&B outfits had followed suit, and before long the Precision bass and the Fender Bassman amplifier with its four 10-in. speakers had taken up residence at the back of the stage in every jumping club from Memphis to Chicago.

below > **Ike Turner's Kings Of Rhythm with their brand-new Fender Strat and Precision bass, 1956.**

timeline

1951 Fender Precision bass launched. Double-cutaway blond-finished ash body with large black Bakelite pickguard, maple neck and fingerboard, narrow Telecaster-style headstock, single-coil pickup.

1954 Body beveled to match Stratocaster design, with sunburst finish and white pickguard.

1955 Staggered-height polepieces, steel bridge saddles replace pressed fiber.

1957 New split-design pickup, strings anchor at bridge instead of rear of body, new shape anodized aluminum pickguard, new Strat-style headstock.

1959 Slab rosewood fingerboard replaces maple. White pickguard changes to imitation tortoiseshell or laminated white/black/white on custom-color models.

1962 Curved rosewood fingerboard.

1963 Thin "veneer" rosewood fingerboard.

1968 Optional maple neck with glued-on maple fingerboard.

1969 Optional one-piece maple neck.

1976 Thumbrest moves to bass side.

above top > **The 1957/1958 Precision Bass adopted the Stratocaster's body contours and headstock profile, but added a new split pickup and an anodized aluminum pickguard.**

right > **By the 1960s the Precision had again followed the lead of the Jazzmaster and Strat by adding a rosewood fingerboard. This Lake Placid Blue example has its original pickup cover and "ashtray" bridge cover intact.**

the fender telecaster   pure simplicity

In 1948, in terms of guitar design, Gibson's old headquarters in Kalamazoo, Michigan, and Fender's Fullerton plant in California's Orange County could have been on different planets: in Kalamazoo, Gibson were slowly and carefully developing the 20-year old archtop guitar for the electric age; in California, Leo Fender and his partner George Fullerton were looking at the electric guitar from a new, fresh angle. Fender had already made some excellent Hawaiian-style lap steels and some good-sounding amplifiers. Now Leo Fender aimed his engineering expertise at the solid-body electric guitar.

While Gibson, Epiphone, Gretsch, and others offered halfway effective solutions to the electric problem, Leo Fender carried on asking questions. Why should a guitar have an expensive arched top? Why glue necks to bodies when four screws would do the job perfectly well? Why separate the bridge and the pickup housing units? Why do all pegheads have three tuners on each side? By 1950, aiming straight for easy, effective production, Fender had become the first manufacturer to put the solid-body electric Spanish guitar into production.

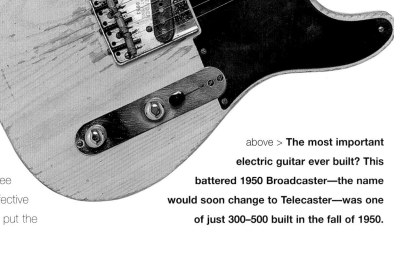

above > **The most important electric guitar ever built? This battered 1950 Broadcaster—the name would soon change to Telecaster—was one of just 300–500 built in the fall of 1950.**

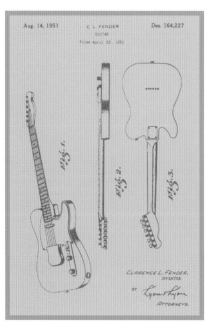

far left > **Total treble: for hot guitarists like Clarence "Gatemouth" Brown, the Telecaster was the answer to their dreams.**

left > **Leo Fender's original patent, filed in April 1951, depicts a guitar that is instantly recognizable as the Telecaster we know today.**

the tele sound

The heart of the Fender Esquire—soon renamed the Broadcaster, then the Telecaster, after Gretsch claimed copyright to the name Broadkaster—was the single-coil pickup designed by Leo Fender and his early partner Doc Kaufman for use on their Hawaiian guitars. This pickup had six polepieces, one for each string. The pickup shared its housing with the bridgeplate giving the Telecaster a sharp, super-steely sound. Early examples had just one pickup. Before long "Esquire" became the name for the single-pickup model, while twin-pickup models were called Telecasters.

On these earliest examples the "tone" control is actually a "mixer" control, while the selector switch acts both as a pickup selector and as a tone selector for the rhythm pickup, giving a range of warm, deep sounds for strummed rhythm backing or country-style basslines. The timbers—ash for the body and maple for the neck—provided tons of sustain and accentuated the new guitar's attacking sound, a combination of woody warmth and pure, trebly Hawaiian-style electric tone.

below > **Industrial design: the Telecaster's innovative bolt-together construction was integral to its tough, steely sound.**

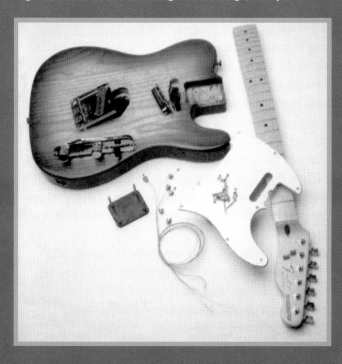

identifier

telecasters in the 1950s

Fender's new guitar debuted in 1950, with single-pickup Esquires costing $139.95. By 1951, the twin-pickup version, now named the Telecaster, was on sale for $169.95.

the bolt-on neck design was quick to manufacture and made the Telecaster easy to adjust and repair.

bodies of prototypes were made of lightweight pine, but the production guitars were made from a simple, two- or three-piece slab of ash.

early guitars were sometimes painted black, but the standard finish was a modern see-through buttermilk-yellow shade known as "blond."

the innovative neck did not carry a separate rosewood or ebony fingerboard: instead, the frets were set directly into the maple itself.

the bridge was a design masterpiece, performing multiple tasks. Screwed firmly to the body for maximum stability, it fed the strings in through the rear of the body, provided three separate saddles, as seen above, to offer increased control over string height and intonation, and acted as a mounting for the treble pickup.

the neck pickup screwed directly into the body itself, while a black Bakelite pickguard covered the body routing and protected the finish.

the tele and the blues
the future for guitars

The instrument industry might have scoffed at the new Fender guitar, but players knew the Telecaster represented the future. A solid body gave players freedom from feedback: the pickups on a solid Fender guitar might squeal a little if you walked right up to a full-volume amplifier, but that was about it. Another advantage was toughness; a blow that would destroy a semi-acoustic guitar would only chip a Fender's lacquer, and at worst a Telecaster's neck could be replaced in a matter of minutes.

After only minor changes and tweaks over the first few years, the biggest turn-around came in 1959, when Fender dropped the all-maple neck for a new design with an old-fashioned rosewood fingerboard. The basic concept, however, stayed exactly the same...a sign that Fender had got the Telecaster almost perfect from the word go.

above > **Scarlet fever: By the 1960s the Telecaster came with a rosewood fingerboard, a three-ply scratchplate, and in a stunning array of custom colors.**

"I wouldn't use anything but the Telecaster with Booker T. and the MGs. It's the sound. I used to use a Super Reverb amp—the extra midrange is right for that guitar. No effects...just plug in and go." steve cropper

left > **The Telecaster Custom and Esquire Custom's "startling new look" was in fact a bid for the traditionalists' market, the only difference being unnecessary but attractive double body binding.**

identifier

blues telecasters

To get up on stage and deliver the sharp, pure sound of a Telecaster you had to know what you were doing. Initially the Tele made the biggest splash among professional country players—names like Johnny Cash's Luther Perkins, Buck Owens and his guitarist Don Rich, plus Waylon Jennings, Merle Haggard, and Willie Nelson. Blues guitarists tendency to crank up their amps made the Tele's ear-splitting character an even braver choice.

Still, many players made the jump from amplified archtops and never looked back. B. B. King played a 1950s Esquire years before he became associated with semi-solid Gibsons. Hot Texas guitarist Clarence "Gatemouth" Brown played a Telecaster in the early 1950s; and over at Stax records in Memphis a few years later, the superbly minimalist young R&B picker Steve Cropper would nail some of the best Tele tones of all time. New Orleans's walking jukebox Snooks Eaglin also sometimes plays an early 1960s Tele.

below > **The ever-tasteful Stax Records house guitarist Steve Cropper with his early 1960s Telecaster.**

dating guide

Fender guitars often have their date of manufacture penciled inside the neck pocket or under the scratchplate in a body rout. Later models usually have a stamp on the end of the neck showing the year, month, and style of neck of the guitar. Telecasters from 1950 to 1954 have a serial number on the bridgeplate; those from 1954 to 1976 show the number on the neckplate. From 1976 the number appears on the peghead decal until 1982, when the number shifted back to the neckplate. Without access to a serial number, a Telecaster or Esquire can often be dated by checking its features. Here are some of the main changes up to the first USA re-issues of 1982:

bridge pickup Flush polepieces until 1955, flat ones afterward.

neck Maple fingerboard until 1959, rosewood 1959–1983, maple option 1967–1969.

pickguard Five-screw single-laminate black to 1954, white plastic 1954 onward, eight screws from 1959, laminated white/black/white from 1963, laminated black/white/black 1975–1981.

string guides One until 1972, two afterward.

bridge Brass saddles 1950–1954, nonthreaded steel saddles 1955–1958, threaded steel saddles late 1958. Strings anchored at bridge in 1959 only.

controls Dome-topped knobs and barrel-shaped switch until 1955, flatter knobs and top-hat switch 1955 onward.

headstock Gold or silver "spaghetti" decal 1950–1967; bolder "transition" logo 1967; black logo 1968; new silver/black logo, 1983.

muddy waters **electrifying the blues**

Muddy Waters' music was a primal howl that literally saved the blues. Through the 1940s and early 1950s the blues had become light, jazzy entertainment. Had Waters not galvanized the Chicago blues scene, bringing it back to its original raw Delta roots, the best work of John Lee Hooker, Howlin' Wolf, and Elmore James might never have reached a wide audience. Without Waters, the Rolling Stones, Jimi Hendrix, and Eric Clapton would have had no idol—and rock'n'roll would have taken a completely different path.

Born McKinley Morganfield in Rolling Fork, Mississippi in 1915, Waters grew up on the Stovall plantation in the heart of Delta blues country. As a youngster he encountered the cream of local blues musicians: Son House, Robert Johnson, and Robert Nighthawk, plus harmonica player Sonny Boy Williamson II and Robert Lockwood Jr., one of the very first blues guitarists to turn electric. The young Waters played traditional acoustic blues, and it was this early style that folklorist Alan Lomax recorded in 1941.

Waters hooked up with guitarist Jimmy Rogers in Chicago, 1943, and played clubs and house parties. He backed up piano player Sunnyland Slim, recorded his first single, "Gypsy Woman," and formed a small band with Rogers and harp-blower Little Walter creating a unique method of blending rhythm and lead guitar they called "fillin' in the cracks." Their 1948 recordings of "I Can't Be Satisfied" and "Feel Like Goin' Home," were vibrant, direct, and confident, while their fabulous

1950 cuts—"Hoochie Coochie Man," "Got My Mojo Working," and "Mannish Boy"—heralded a whole new style of blues.

Muddy Waters and his band were the kings of Chicago through the 1950s, and as the black audience began to move toward soul and R&B, Waters gained a new, white audience by recording his 1963 *Folk Singer* album with the young Buddy Guy on acoustic guitar, and enjoyed continuing success up to his death in 1983.

Among Muddy Waters's achievements was the rough, urban Chicago blues style, linking the original down home Delta style with rock'n'roll. He fostered the very best musicians; he introduced folk and jazz audiences to real blues; and he left a legacy of great tunes that still get the dancefloor shaking today.

right > **Muddy Waters pitched for the acoustic blues market in 1960 with an album of Broonzy cover versions.**

slide master

As the most influential blues bandleader of all, Muddy Waters was also a wild guitar player. In his early career he played a Gretsch archtop fitted with a DeArmond pickup and a goldtop Les Paul, but his Telecaster, bought new in 1957, has become one of the most famous guitars in blues history. Waters named his guitar "Hoss," (right), changed the color from white to metallic red, and swapped the neck for a wider version with a rosewood fingerboard in 1961. He also added extra screws to keep the scratchplate down, and swapped the knurled metal knobs for black plastic Fender amp knobs. Waters strung his Tele with medium-gauge 0.012–0.056 Gibson strings with an unwound third, set the action high, and used a metal thumbpick and fingerpick on his right hand and a short metal slide on his left hand little finger. He often employed a capo, but rarely tuned his guitar to anything but standard tuning. He played through a 40-watt Fender Super Reverb with four 10-inch speakers, using neither reverb nor tremolo, and set the volume at 9, controlling the overall level from the guitar.

telecaster **variations on a theme**

Down the years Fender has tried hard to update the Telecaster. In 1959 the company introduced the Telecaster Custom, and in 1968 the semi-hollow-bodied Thinline, the Rosewood Telecaster, a super-heavy model played by George Harrison, and the psychedelic Paisley Telecaster. In 1970 it edged closer toward the Gibson approach with the Custom Telecaster.

For most guitarists, though, the only real Tele remains the Tele pure and simple, a straightforward solid body with those two great single-coil pickups. Dozens of satisfied users—including James Burton, Jimmy Page, Keith Richards, Danny Gatton, Roy Buchanan, Eric Clapton, Jeff Beck in the Yardbirds, Clarence White, and Robben Ford—attest to the fact that there's not much wrong with the basic recipe.

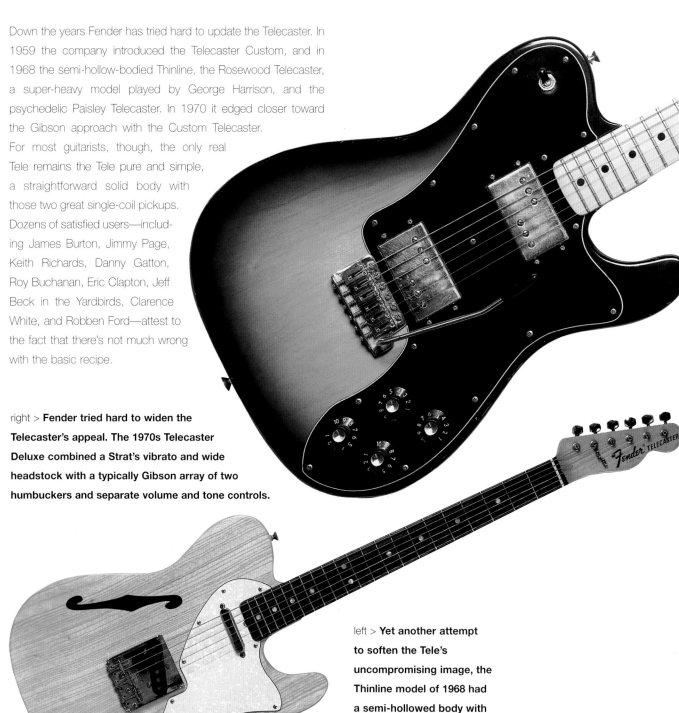

right > **Fender tried hard to widen the Telecaster's appeal. The 1970s Telecaster Deluxe combined a Strat's vibrato and wide headstock with a typically Gibson array of two humbuckers and separate volume and tone controls.**

left > **Yet another attempt to soften the Tele's uncompromising image, the Thinline model of 1968 had a semi-hollowed body with an old-fashioned f-hole.**

right > **The Iceman: Texas Telecaster master Albert Collins installed a humbucker in the neck position.**

identifier

albert collins

They called Albert Collins "The Iceman" for his cold, sharp tone, and he played up to his name with albums like *Ice Cold Blues*, *Frostbite*, and *Cold Snap*. Born in 1932 in Leona, Texas, Collins was one of fiercest, most unorthodox blues players of all time, with cool guitar instrumentals that rivaled Freddie King's. Though heavily influenced by other Texas pickers like Guitar Slim, T-Bone Walker, Lowell Fulson, and Gatemouth Brown, Collins formed his own style by playing swinging, organ-like blues/funk finger-style licks on a 1961 Telecaster, customized with extra binding and a neck humbucker, and played at hellish volume through a Fender Quad Reverb amp cranked all the way to 10. He employed a highly unusual minor tuning—generally an open E or F—and used a capo extensively, sometimes as high as the seventh or eighth fret.

Times turned hard after his 1958 hit "Freeze," and Collins spent much of the 1960s mixing car paint. He enjoyed a spell on the rock concert circuit with the help of fans Canned Heat, but gave up playing from 1972 to 1979. In the 1980s he was back, recording an excellent album, *Collins Mix*, and guesting with John Lee Hooker, Gary Moore, B. B. King, and his number one fan Robert Cray. Collins died of cancer tragically early in 1993, at the age of 61. Despite his name, The Iceman was one of the hottest things ever to come out of Texas.

fender's blues teles

Since 1982 Fender has done its best to please fans of the original Telecaster by including accurate reproductions of 1950s maple-neck and 1960s rosewood-neck Telecasters in its range. Other subtle updates include the American Standard Tele, an all-round favorite since 1986, and the Set-Neck Tele, an all-mahogany glued-neck variation with fat-sounding single-coils based on vintage DeArmond pickups.

Committed fans can even buy Telecasters that aim to replicate every nuance of a famous blues player's guitar, like the off-the-shelf customized Albert Collins Telecaster. One of Fender's best-ever "signature" guitars is the Muddy Waters Telecaster, a Custom Shop repro of Waters's much-altered 1957 model, complete with extra-wide neck, extra screws securing the scratchplate, and skirted amp knobs in place of the usual metal versions. But you'll have to supply for yourself the man's howling bottleneck sound.

right > **The mid-priced Mexican-made Fender Muddy Waters Telecaster comes in Candy Apple Red with special pickups, amp-style knobs, and a chunky neck with a slab rosewood fingerboard.**

the fender bassman
sound of the blues

Some of the greatest blues guitarists swore by Gibson amps, Magnatones or even cheap, cheerful Silvertones, but Fenders soon became the working player's amplifier of choice. They were tough, they were roadworthy, and when you rolled the volume hard right they gave you piles of volume and searing, gritty sustain—a by-product of Leo Fender's policy of pushing tube specifications to their limits. Tubes in Fenders didn't last as long as in some other amps, but the results were worth it: Buddy Guy, Otis Rush, and many other Chicago blues stars used Fender Bassman amps in the 1950s.

With a super-hot preamp, tube rectification for a smooth, player-sensitive response, Middle and Presence controls, two inputs per channel, and four 10-inch Jensen speakers, the 40-watt Bassman is now widely regarded as the best blues

amp ever made. The Bassman had originally been launched in 1952 with a 15-inch speaker to partner the Precision Bass, but when in 1955 Fender altered the circuitry and added four Jensen P10Rs, word soon spread that the Bassman made a fabulous, fat-sounding guitar amplifier. The finest models of all were made in 1959, with a 5F6A circuit that connected the negative feedback loop to the phase inverter, enhancing the presence control. This was the amplifier virtually copied by Jim Marshall, Ken Bran, and Dudley Craven in London, in 1962, to create the Marshall JTM45, the basis for the staggering sound made by Eric Clapton in his Bluesbreaker days of the mid 1960s.

right > **The tweed Bassman was specifically designed as a bass amplifier, but blues players discovered that it worked even better as a guitar amp. This is a '59 Bassman reissue.**

back to the future

Players' growing fascination with the never-bettered blues tones of the 1950s led Fender to introduce the first-ever "re-issue" amplifier in 1990—and, of course, it chose the charismatic tweed-covered Bassman. Though Fender kept costs down by using modern components and printed circuit boards, and although re-issue Jensens were at this time unavailable, the 1959 Bassman re-issue provided a fine approximation of the original's fiery sound. Before long, smaller specialist companies like Kendrick, Victoria, THD, Holland, and many others, had begun making even closer copies, hand-wired throughout and with solid pine cabinets just like the old ones, with specially developed vintage-toned 10-inch drivers.

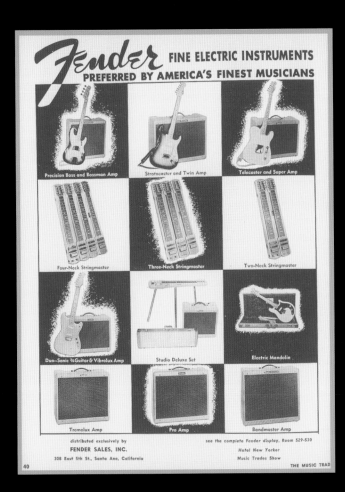

above > **Fender's ads suggested pairing the Strat with the Twin Amp and the Tele with the Super Amp.**

identifier

fender's tweed amps

Though the Bassman was the blues king, Fender's other tweed amplifiers were also widely used:

15-watt dual professional

Launched in 1946 and was intended as a steel guitar amp but its two 10-inch speakers made it a fine standard guitar amp, too. The amp was renamed the Super and launched as a partner for the Telecaster in 1951.

the 15-watt twin amp entered the line in 1952 with two 12-inch speakers, and an extra tube in the preamp stage.

deluxe A lower-powered design, it is still favored today as a top recording amp.

the bandmaster was essentially a Bassman but with three 10-inch speakers instead of four. Like Bassmans, they fetch high prices in today's market.

15-watt tremolux Sacrificed overall output for the sake of a pulsating "tremolo" effect. The Vibrolux was a smaller relation, delivering 10 watts into a single 10-inch speaker.

top > **The "wide panel" Deluxe was made from 1952 until 1956. Though low-powered, it's considered one of the finest-sounding Fender combos.**
above > **After covering their amps in luggage tweed, Fender moved to brown and cream Tolex, then black. This late-model Twin Amp was Fender's top-line guitar combo before the advent of the Twin Reverb.**

the dawn of reverb
fender's echo effect

Fender ushered in the 1960s with a brand new sound: reverb. This classic Fender effect is produced by a spring reverb unit, an electromechanical device in which the incoming signal is fed through a transducer, then into a sealed box containing springs. The sound is transmitted down the springs and received on the other side of the unit after a slight delay, where it is converted back into an electrical signal. This "wet" signal is then mixed and re-amplified back into the circuit in the desired proportions, to give an echo effect. Fender first offered the reverb as a stand-alone unit in 1961, but over the next few years it became standard on most of its larger combos.

The Twin Reverb amp, Fender's new all-conquering design, used four 6L6 output tubes to give around 80 watts of power (100 watts in later models), and was notoriously loud. As PA systems in the 1960s were generally reserved for amplifying vocals, harmonicas, and brass instruments, guitar players needed all the volume they could get. Fender's powerful models like the Twin Reverb and Dual Showman provided exactly that. Muddy Waters and Otis Rush both used a 40-watt Super Reverb, and even in the 1980s Stevie Ray Vaughan based his sound around Super Reverbs and a 2 x 10 inch Vibrolux Reverb.

below > **The compact 22-watt Deluxe Reverb lacks the clean headroom of the Twin Reverb, but its fine-sounding natural overdrive makes it one of the most sought-after blackface Fender combos today.**

below > **Recording king: the Princeton Reverb.**

"In 1969 I saw Philip Guy, Buddy Guy's brother, playing a Strat through a Fender Super Reverb with just the right shimmering of echo on it. It sounded like someone had thrown a rock across a frozen lake—the coolest sound I'd ever heard. I thought, man, I've got to get one of those..." robert cray

hot dates

Fender amps of the 1950s or 1960s can be dated in three ways. A date code on the tube chart stuck on the inside gives two letters: the first runs from A in 1951 through to O in 1965. The second letter is the month, starting with A in January. This date can be cross-referenced with the 6-digit code stamped on the speaker chassis. Jensen codes start with 220, Oxfords with 465. The fourth digit indicates the year, the last two the week of the year. A code 220519, therefore, indicates a Jensen from the nineteenth week of 1955—or possibly 1965. Finally, potentiometers also have 6- or 7-digit date codes. Again, the first three indicate the manufacturer and the last three the year and week of the year in which the pot was made. Checking the amp's features should help identify the correct decade.

below > **Cool combination: Robert Cray with Stratocaster and Fender Super Reverb amp.**

identifier

fender amps of the 1960s

Fender's "blackface" amps are fine blues workhorses, and the later "silverface" equivalents without master volume controls can easily be modified to sound as good:

showman First of the cream-covered "piggy-back" amplifiers, with a choice of 1 x 12-inch or 1 x 15-inch speaker cabinets. The Dual Showman came with a 2 x 12-inch cab.

pro reverb The 2 x 12 inch Pro Reverb is the same physical size as the Twin Reverb, but the 40-watt output is considered more suitable for blues.

super reverb The 1960s equivalent to the 1950s 4 x 10-inch Bassman, the Super is a 40-watt 4 x 10-inch combo with an extra middle control.

vibrolux reverb This was basically a Pro Reverb with slightly less power and two 10-inch speakers.

deluxe reverb With a single 12-inch speaker and two 6V6 output tubes giving around 22 watts of power, the Deluxe Reverb gives sweet overdrive and makes a great small club amp.

bandmaster and bandmaster reverb 40-watt and 45-watt heads designed to partner 2 x 12-inch cabinets.

quad reverb A super-loud 100-watt amp, as used by Albert Collins, running into a 4 x 12-inch cab—or, in the case of the Super Six model, a 6 x 10-inch version—and in "silverface" only.

top right > **A 1970s "silverface" Dual Showman Reverb.**
above > **The Pro Reverb is much the same size and weight as the Twin Reverb, but its lower 40-watt output gives better break-up at club volumes.**

solid gold, easy action
the gibson les paul

"It's a sensation!" said Gibson's copywriters, and for once they were right as 1952 saw the launch of a guitar that would eventually power a whole new blues style. The sound of Michael Bloomfield, Eric Clapton, Peter Green, and Jimmy Page was the sound of a Gibson guitar with high output pickups and fitted with skinny, easy-to-bend strings, amplified through a Fender or a Marshall. At least, that's the accepted history. In truth, however, black American blues musicians were among the very first guitarists to pick up on the latest trend. Publicity photos from around 1953 and 1954 tellingly show brand-new Les Pauls already in the hands of the cream of contemporary blues guitarists including John Lee Hooker, Muddy Waters, and Guitar Slim. Buddy Guy played a Les Paul in the 1950s, as did Howlin' Wolf's guitarists Hubert Sumlin and Jody Williams.

above > **One of the first-ever Gibson Les Paul Models from 1952. The design was considered so radical that at one point Gibson were considering not even putting their name on the guitar.**

After the appearance of the Fender Telecaster, Gibson knew it could design and make a guitar to out-shoot the Fender, which one Gibson employee scornfully described as "the plank." Under the direction of Ted McCarty, Gibson's draftsmen drew up plans for a guitar designed to combine the best of the company's famous old-world craftsmanship with a solid body, its subtle outline derived from a sharp-cutaway archtop guitar. Indeed, the new guitar was also designed from the outset to include an arched top: Gibson was sure that Fender didn't have the machinery to do the same. What Gibson wasn't sure about was whether players would accept a Gibson solid-body electric—or even if such a move risked damaging the company's reputation.

right > **A pre-Telecaster Muddy Waters, pictured around 1954.**

sound secrets

Gibson hit on a magic formula for the Les Paul: a body of mahogany, capped with a carved maple top. Solid maple had proved too heavy; mahogany and maple gave the right combination of weight and sustain, and Les Paul's ideas for a showy gold finish hid the timber combination from prying eyes. The pickups Gibson chose were single-coil P-90s, the best units available to them at the time. The sound of the new guitar was fat and loud, as exemplified by "Hideaway" and "The Stumble," the Freddie King instrumentals so beloved of the young British blues-boomers in the early 1960s.

below > **Chess recording artist "Little" Milton Campbell with his Les Paul.**

identifier

the early les paul goldtop

finish The Les Paul Model, introduced in mid 1952, came with a radical gold top. Gibson also made some "all-gold" examples with the gold finish extending to cover the entire body and back of the neck.

the neck and main body section were made of Honduras mahogany, while the arched top was made of three pieces of unmatched maple.

the bridge/tailpiece was originally a large trapeze-type affair, but this was rapidly phased out in favor of a wraparound stud bridge/tailpiece.

pickups were P-90s in cream-colored "soapbar" covers. Some early examples had black pickup covers and unbound fingerboards.

serial numbers The first Les Pauls had no serial numbers. By 1953, serial numbers appeared on the back of the headstock.

right > **Gibson replaced the ill-advised "trapeze" bridge/tailpiece with a simple, great-sounding but only partially adjustable "stud" type in mid 1953. On the Les Paul Model this bridge lasted just two years until the Tune-O-Matic was introduced in late 1955.**

gilding the lily the goldtop and the custom

Gibson's aim with the Les Paul was to convince electric archtop-players that the solid-body was the way of the future. It held two cards: the quality Gibson name; and the design itself, a brilliant combination of the traditional and the new. But Gibson needed a figurehead and it found one in Les Paul, a professional player and gifted inventor. Les Paul liked the idea of the new guitar and he worked with Gibson until the Les Paul Model was ready for production in 1952.

The first guitars had problems. Gibson followed Les Paul's suggestion for a special all-in-one combined bridge and tailpiece, but set the neck into the body at too flat an angle, requiring the strings to wrap under, not over, the new bridge/tailpiece. Les Paul complained that this interfered with the player's right-hand technique, and by 1953 the system was changed for a simple stud bridge/tail-piece, allowing conventional string-damping and certainly improving sustain still further. It was a success: Gibson sold over 4,000 Les Pauls in the first two years of production.

above > **1957 was the last year of the original Les Paul gold finish, but the first year for the wide-sounding humbuckers and the fully adjustable Tune-O-Matic bridge.**

right > **John Lee Hooker with a Les Paul, mid 1950s.**

"I'm sure Freddie King didn't mind us playing his music. . . but I don't think there was any problem with us emulating his instrumentals."

fleetwood mac's peter green

identifier

freddie king

When the young Eric Clapton spotted a gold Les Paul on the cover of an early Freddie King album, he knew it was the guitar for him. Born in Gilmer, Texas in 1934, King was among the very first black guitarists to cross over to the new white audience with a selection of sharp, hip records. Weighing in at 250 lb (550 kg) and over six feet (1.8 m) tall, King packed a double whammy: an extrovert Texas fingerpicking guitar style—think Gatemouth Brown or Albert Collins—with a Chicago-tinged vocal approach that echoed B. B. King and Buddy Guy. In King's own words, he played "like Louis Jordan used to play his horn." In the 1960s King took up a Gibson ES-345 that he played through a Fender Showman set to maximum treble and at a shattering volume, and made his name with the 1961 all-instrumental album Let's Hide Away And Dance Away. Songs like "Hide Away," "The Stumble," and "San-Ho-Zay" were a huge success, and King enjoyed a concert-packed career up to his death in 1976.

black beauty

custom In 1954 Gibson introduced the $325 Les Paul Custom, nicknamed the Black Beauty, an ebony-finished high-end alternative to the Les Paul Model.

materials and finish The new guitar was all-mahogany, without a maple cap, and came finished in black with multiple body-binding, gold-plated hardware, a split-diamond headstock inlay and rectangular pearl fingerboard markers.

bridge/tailpiece Where the Les Paul Model had a basic wraparound stud bridge/tailpiece, the Custom featured a stop tailpiece and Gibson's new Tune-O-Matic bridge with adjustable intonation for each string.

frets Gibson fitted special low profile frets, giving rise to the nickname "Fretless Wonder." They also offered a version with a Bigsby vibrato.

pickups The Les Paul Custom carried a P-90 pickup at the bridge and a larger Alnico V version by the neck. In 1957 the model received three latest-design humbucking pickups.

left > **Blues giant: Freddie King was later known for playing thinline Gibson semis but he was pictured with a Les Paul on an influential 1950s album.**

stripped-down sound
the gibson les paul junior

At over $350, the Les Paul was a luxury item. A Fender could be bought for under $200, and Gibson knew it had to capture the lower-end of the guitar market too. Its response, in 1954, was to launch a direct attack on the Fender Esquire with the $120 Les Paul Junior: one pickup, no frills, no trimmings.

But Gibson was Gibson, and it couldn't allow itself to go the whole hog with what they viewed as distinctly inferior screwed-on necks. The Junior contained all the vital ingredients of the Les Paul recipe. It had a body and neck made of Honduras mahogany, one of the finest woods for solid body guitars. It had a traditional rosewood fingerboard and a proper kicked-back Gibson headstock. It even had the same pickup as the Les Paul Model. All it lacked was the carved maple top of the original, and of course the flashy gold finish—but Gibson had an idea there, too, and a year after the Junior's launch a new finish option was added to the basic sunburst, a creamy "limed mahogany." The TV Model, as the guitar with the new look was called, may have been specially designed to show up well on television—or perhaps Gibson was just following Fender's futuristically named Telecaster with a suitably high-tech name. The middle ground was filled with the launch in 1955 of the Les Paul Special, a twin-pickup version of the Junior.

above > **With a flat body, a single P-90 pickup and no frills, the Les Paul Junior was designed as a student guitar. Yellow "TV" models, like this double-cutaway '58, are especially collectable today.**

right > **A 1959 Gibson flyer featuring Les Paul and Mary Ford and four Les Paul models: the black Custom, the sunburst Standard, the "cream finish SGC Special" and the "limed mahogany finish" SG TV, a.k.a. the Les Paul Junior, "a favorite with students and advanced players."**

sound secrets

Vintage Les Paul Juniors have shot up in price as players have come to realize that you can't beat pure simplicity and style. The simple wrap-around stud bridge/tailpiece feeds the vibrations of the strings straight into the body, and with no maple cap, the Junior's one-piece mahogany body with its glued-in mahogany neck makes for a lightweight guitar with a warm but super-sensitive response. Gibson's placing of the single P-90 was perfect, giving a riotously raw lead sound that cleans up beautifully for rhythm work when you lower the pickup's gain by easing back on the volume control. The Les Paul Special has much the same appeal, plus an extra neck pickup for darker, jazzier tones, but it lacks the Junior's brutal, bluesy simplicity.

below > **Last of the breed: a 1961 double-cutaway Les Paul Special in cherry red.**

identifier

timeline

1954 Les Paul Junior introduced with flat, single-cutaway mahogany body, single P-90, wraparound bridge/tailpiece, dot markers and tortoiseshell-style pickguard. Finish: opaque two-tone sunburst.

1955 Les Paul Special introduced. Twin P-90s, two-volume and two-tone controls and three-way switch, bound fingerboard, multi-layered scratchplate and truss rod cover. Finish: limed mahogany (also called "natural" or "limed oak"). Same finish added to Junior model, named "TV finish."

1956 Les Paul Junior ¾ introduced, with 15 frets clear of the body and a 22 ¾ in. scale.

1958 Les Paul Junior and TV both change to double-cutaway body

1959 Les Paul Special also gains double cutaways and an optional cherry finish; switch moves closer to bridge and neck pickup moves away from fingerboard. Special renamed "SG Special," and Les Paul TV "SG TV," though design stays the same.

1961 Les Paul Junior and SG Special both change to twin-horned "SG" design.

right > **From 1955 to 1958, Les Paul Specials followed the single-cutaway format. This one has the limed mahogany finish.**

the standard **the ultimate les paul**

By 1957, after a period of encouraging sales, Gibson saw the popularity of the handsome but heavy Les Paul falling away. Its first move in response to this was to fit the goldtop model with a set of its brand-new humbucking pickups. Its second, in 1958, was to drop the gold finish entirely, and to replace it with a traditional Gibson sunburst laid over a two-piece maple top. Gibson called this the Les Paul Standard. Sales did improve, but not by much, and three years later Gibson would dump the entire Les Paul concept and replace it with the sleeker, lighter SG ("solid guitar") line.

Meanwhile, young bands were busily absorbing Muddy Waters and Freddie King records. Keeping a close eye on the guitars his heroes played, Keith Richard chose a Standard in 1964, but soon swapped it for an Epiphone Casino. The following year, Eric Clapton matched a 1959 Les Paul Standard with a 35-watt Marshall tremolo combo with two Celestion speakers, creating the sound on John Mayall and The Bluesbreakers' *Beano* album. Peter Green, another Bluesbreakers protegee, owned a LP Standard that had been re-assembled wrongly, giving a distinctive out-of-phase sound on the middle selector setting. Before long, Jimmy Page had joined the Les Paul movement, soon to be followed in the States by Duane Allman, and ZZ Top's Billy Gibbons with his famous Les Paul 'burst, Pearly Gates.

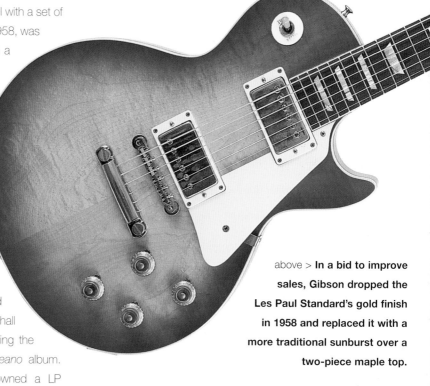

above > **In a bid to improve sales, Gibson dropped the Les Paul Standard's gold finish in 1958 and replaced it with a more traditional sunburst over a two-piece maple top.**

below > **Eric Clapton cemented the cult of the Les Paul Standard when he adopted the model in the mid 1960s.**

identifier

les paul standard factfile

sunburst finish Over a two-piece maple top replaced the goldtop finish in mid 1958.

limited numbers Gibson produced only 1,712 sunburst-finish Les Pauls between 1958 and 1960.

differences Different years have their own followings: examples from 1958 tend have the thickest necks; guitars from 1959 carried new, wider frets, while guitars produced in 1960 have much slimmer necks.

soapbar p-90s Though Gibson hastily re-introduced the Les Paul goldtop in 1968, it had soapbar P-90s—not the 1959-style humbuckers players wanted.

1972–1976 Goldtop Standards at last came with optional humbuckers.

replicas Stung by excellent Far Eastern replicas, Gibson brought back the sunburst Les Paul Standard in 1976, and it has remained in production ever since.

vintage re-issues The first reasonably faithful vintage-style model was the Gibson '59 re-issue of 1985.

current range Gibson's current catalog carries a number of flame-top sunbursts, including the Les Paul Standard, with a choice of 1950s or 1960s necks: the Les Paul Premium Plus; the hot-pickup 1960-style Classic; plus custom-order 1958 and 1960 re-issues, and Custom Authentic versions.

gibson's humbucker

Until the introduction of the Gibson humbucker in 1957, players had to put up with buzz and hum caused by other electrical devices interfering with their single-coil pickups. Gibson's new pickup, designed by Walter Fuller and Seth Lover, had twin coils connected in opposite polarity that drastically reduced hum—and produced a thicker, more powerful sound into the bargain. Early examples, nicknamed "PAFs" after the "Patent Applied For" sticker on the underside, are the most crucial ingredient of the LP Standard's sound. In truth the pickups vary widely, as Gibson's coil-winding machines had no automatic stop facility and commonly overwound the pickups by as much as 20 percent. The PAF debuted on the Les Paul and ES-175 in 1957 and soon spread across Gibson's top-line guitars.

above > **Gibson's new sound: the twin-coil humbucker debuted in 1957.**

left > **Thanks to a rewiring mistake, Peter Green's Les Paul had a distinctive tone when both pickups were switched on.**

vintage guitars   the les paul phenomenon

Mike Bloomfield was one of the very the first white electric blues cult figures. Born in Chicago in 1944, one-time chauffeur for Big Joe Williams, Bloomfield learned his trade in the clubs of Chicago's West Side. By the mid 1960s he had teamed up with harpist Paul Butterfield, and shared lead duties with Elvin Bishop on the hard-rocking album *The Paul Butterfield Blues Band* (1965). The album sleeve showed Bloomfield clutching a 1952 Telecaster—and prices for original Telecasters skyrocketed virtually overnight. Later, Bloomfield took up a goldtop Les Paul and then a sunburst Les Paul Standard, and the same thing happened. For the first time, stars were rejecting new guitars in favor of used, often discontinued models. It was the beginning of the vintage electric guitar craze.

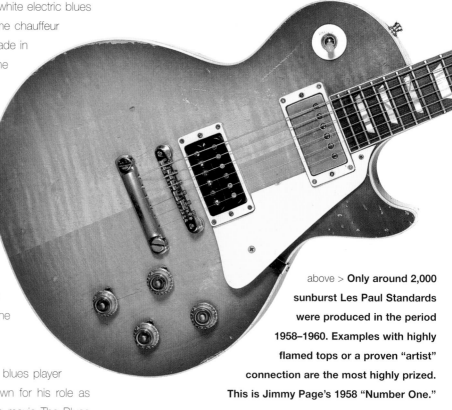

above > **Only around 2,000 sunburst Les Paul Standards were produced in the period 1958–1960. Examples with highly flamed tops or a proven "artist" connection are the most highly prized. This is Jimmy Page's 1958 "Number One."**

A fine example of the new breed of Les Paul blues player was Matt "Guitar" Murphy. He was best known for his role as Aretha Franklin's long-suffering husband in the movie The Blues Brothers, but Matt "Guitar" Murphy also played hot, jazzy blues guitar on many great records. Born in 1927 in Mississippi, Murphy moved to Memphis where he sat in with Howlin' Wolf, Little Junior Parker, and Bobby Bland before hooking up with Memphis Slim and supplying guitar on his fabulous 1950s Vee-Jay releases. In the 1960s Murphy played shows with Chuck Berry, Otis Rush, and Sonny Boy Williamson, and wowed European audiences with a dazzling "Matt's Guitar Boogie" at the American Folk Blues Festival in 1963 (Freddie King once admitted he used Matt's playing as the basis for his famous "Hideaway"). Matt Murphy is still mixing up the funk, the blues, and the jazz, often with his brother Floyd on second guitar. Though he started out on a Fender Esquire, Matt has also played Gibson thinline semi-acoustics. He currently uses a Les Paul Standard re-issue through a Fender Blues DeVille.

right > **In his later years, Freddie King sometimes played a 1970s Les Paul Deluxe with smaller Epiphone-style humbuckers.**

identifier

luther allison

High-octane Les Paul bluesman Luther Allison was born in Arkansas, but honed his music by sitting in with Muddy Waters, Elmore James and Howlin' Wolf in the clubs of Chicago. In 1972 he became the first blues artist to sign to Motown. Later he made his base in France, becoming one of Europe's leading blues stars. By adding elements of reggae, soul, rock, and funk, he preferred to take the music forward than just reproduce the sounds of yesterday. Before he passed away in 1997, just a year after winning five WC Handy blues awards, Allison's signature guitar was "Golden Boy"—a 1960 Goldtop re-issue.

below > **Luther Allison and Golden Boy in full flight.**

A combination of the finest woods, great pickups, quality construction, and considerable rarity makes the 1958–1960 Les Paul Standard the Stradivarius of the electric guitar world. Some guitars carry almost plain maple tops, while others exhibit outrageous flame and "curl" effects. For a collector, the quality of the maple figuring makes all the difference in terms of desirability. By the 1970s, 'Bursts—as they had become known— were fetching over $2000 apiece, and a decade later their price had crept up to around $5,000. Today, a particularly beautiful example might fetch $200,000, and Bloomfield's original Les Paul is rumored to have changed hands for a quarter of a million. American icon the Les Paul Sunburst may be, but it's hard to reconcile art-market prices with the spirit of the blues.

kay guitars blues from the wish book

In the 1950s mail-order guitars were just as important to impoverished musicians as they had been in the 1920s and 1930s. The war was over, good times were around the corner, and America wanted music. With music stores still a rarity outside the cities, dreamers again flipped through the catalogs of Sears (nicknamed "the wish book"), Montgomery Ward, J. C. Penney, and Spiegel's.

Kay guitars had been stalwarts of the prewar scene, first in the 1920s as Stromberg-Voisinet, then in the 1930s as Kay Kraft. After being sold in 1955, Kay's new owners pushed the brand quickly into the electric market. The new Kay guitars would become favorites of the Chicago blues scene and beyond. While a top-of-the-line Kay-built semi-acoustic could cost as much as $400, the same as a Gibson, you could find a great-looking and funky-sounding guitar for less than half that price. Kay built a huge new factory in 1963 to cash in on the latest guitar boom, but struggled to match the prices of the first imported Japanese instruments. Kay was sold in 1965, then again in 1967, this time to guitar-making rival Valco, but Valco would go bust by 1968, taking a great American brand with them.

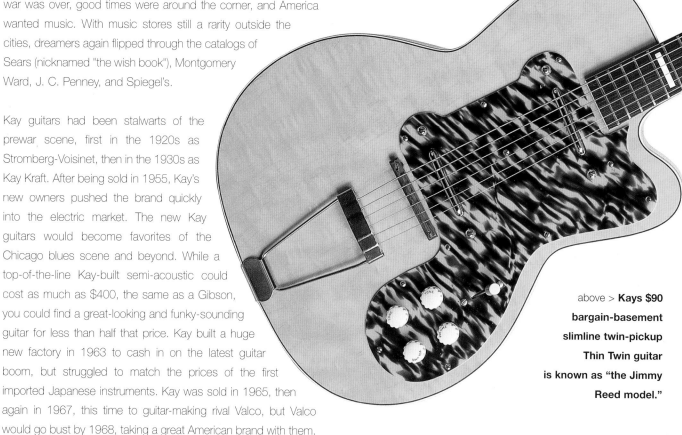

above > **Kays $90 bargain-basement slimline twin-pickup Thin Twin guitar is known as "the Jimmy Reed model."**

right and left > **Howlin' Wolf with a Kay Thin Twin, early 1950s. So many players used these Kays that it's almost as if they all shared one for photo sessions—but close inspection reveals a different guitar each time.**

identifier

jimmy reed

Kay Thin Twin player Jimmy Reed was born Mathis James Reed in Dunleith, Mississippi in 1925. After heading north to Chicago in 1943, he cut a succession of huge-selling blues/pop records for the fledgling Vee-Jay label from 1950 to 1960. Songs like "Big Boss Man," and "Bright Lights, Big City" never had the driving intensity of Howlin' Wolf and Muddy Waters, but Reed's swampy, easygoing shuffle style and loose, drawled vocals made these blues as catchy as influenza; everyone played Jimmy Reed songs, from beginners to Elvis Presley to Rod Stewart. Reed could have been the biggest-ever blues success, but tales of his drinking are legendary. His alcoholism delayed the diagnosis of epilepsy, and though he cleaned up his act Reed passed away on the verge of a comeback in 1976— a tragic end for the ordinary people's favorite bluesman.

below > **Jimmy Reed used various Kay guitars. Here he's playing a three-pickup solid body with a maple fingerboard.**

kays of the 1950s

Low on output and sustain but high on charm, twang, and vibe, a 1950's Kay semi-acoustic was the working man's Gretsch.

the flashy headstocks with their injection-molded plastic facings are known as "Kelvinators" after the logo of the refrigerator manufacturer, while the pickups are nicknamed "Kleenex" types because of the oval aperture on the pickup casings.

the jazz II model as played by Eric Clapton around 1963 in one of his first bands, The Roosters, was a thinline blond semi-acoustic with double rounded cutaways, twin pickups, and a Bigsby vibrato.

barney kessel models Among other sought-after Kays, these were endorsed by the famous jazz and session guitarist.

barney kessel jazz special Spruce-topped, at $400, and Kay's most upmarket electric.

the barney kessel artist, shown right, was a $300 model with a spruce top and a rounded cutaway.

the pro at $200, had a smaller body with no f-holes and a solid center block to minimize feedback.

upbeat A simpler version of the BK Artist in black, with one, two, or three pickups.

sweet harmony **the chicago sound**

Harmony's output dwarfs that of all other American guitar makers: even in the 1930s, it was reporting sales of half a million instruments each year. During World War Two Harmony moved to a new facility in Chicago, and by the 1950s it was producing a range of affordable yet worthy electric guitars.

Semi-acoustics made up a large part of Harmony's electric lineup, with the style slowly evolving from Gretsch-influenced to more mainstream Gibson. The long-lasting Rocket series came with one, two, or three DeArmond-designed pickups built by Rowe Manufacturing, who also provided electronics for Kay. At between $100 and $150, Harmony Rockets were cool, usable budget guitars. The Meteor models offered various upgrades over the Rockets such as fancier hardware and pearl block fingerboard inlays. There was a series of fancy set-neck, deep-bodied jazz guitars to rival the Kay Barney Kessels, including the top-line Artist Jazz and the rare Espanada, with genuine aluminum body binding. The 1960s "H" series Meteors aped Gibson's 335, with thinline double-cutaway bodies and three pickups linked to huge selector switches (and just to hedge its bet, Harmony started adding Fender-style single-sided headstocks to some models). There was even an early attempt at a guitar with built-in effects, the H66 Vibrajet, with a battery-powered tremolo.

left > **This cheap and cheerful Harmony Stratotone Jupiter H-49 was made in 1960. Many Chicago-made guitars had unusual electronics: this model has an extra tone control specifically for the middle position of the three-way pickup selector.**

left > **The Harmony H-75 semi-acoustic didn't sound much like a Gibson...but the toggle switches were huge.**

identifier

elmore james

Born in 1918 in Richland, Mississippi, Elmore James was the most influential and most copied electric slide guitarist of the postwar period. James used cheap, basic guitars, either a flat-top acoustic with an added pickup or a Kay K-125 solid-body, and played simplified, mesmeric Delta bottleneck licks at searing volume. A radio repairman in his spare time, he modified his own amplifiers to create a raging, distorted sound that foreshadowed the blues/rock of Eric Clapton, Jimmy Page, Johnny Winter, Duane Allman, and many others. James's most famous song and most-imitated lick was "Dust My Broom." It was the young guitarist's first recording: he was so shy that he ran away before hearing the playback. After the song had become a hit in 1951, James moved from Memphis to Chicago, where he formed The Broomdusters, one of the Windy City's most feared and respected blues combos. James died in 1963 of a heart attack, and his memorial was attended by hundreds of musicians and fans.

harmony's solid-bodies

Harmony catered for solid-body fans, too:

stratotone series Introduced in 1953 with a diminutive solidbody guitar, the gold-colored H44.

1958 Stratotone changed to a semi-solid design which married a Gibson Les Paul single-cutaway shape with a Telecaster-like flat body. Most carry an "atomic" decoration on the pickguard or headstock.

stratotones came with anything between one and three pickups, plus many control variations. Sears sold tens of thousands under the Silvertone brand.

mercury and jupiter Similar to the semi-solid Stratotones, with hollow bodies but no f-holes.

1960s silhouette series True solid-bodies, with a design that recalled Fender's Jazzmaster.

some silhouettes' vibratos were made by Hagstrom in Sweden, while the ornate single-coil Golden Tone pickups were designed by DeArmond and made by Rowe. These guitars sound great, but extra-thick necks limit their appeal.

left > **Elmore James used a bottom-dollar Kay K-125 electric.**

danelectros and silvertones
the lipstick sound

Cheap, funky, and available in a wide range of futuristic colors from coral red and royal blue to surf green, Danelectro guitars were affordable and remarkably effective. The company was founded in 1947 by Nathan Daniel, an electronics expert who in 1954 turned from making amps to instruments. He first introduced a solid electric guitar with a "peanut"-shaped body and then, in 1956, a range of guitars that would become budget classics: the single-cutaway U1, U2, and U3 models. In 1958 the Danelectro body design changed to the ultra-modern double-cutaway "shorthorn" design, and, in 1959, to a "longhorn" style of guitars and basses.

Danelectro manufactured guitars under its own name, but in the 1950s it also sold thousands through Sears, Roebuck, re-badged as Silvertones. The famous "amp in case" guitar was a short-scaled beginners' favorite, with a hard case that opened to reveal a simple, 3-watt amplifier—a first taste of the electric sound for hundreds of budding guitarists. At the other end of the scale Danelectro also made a number of spectacular double-neck guitars...as played by Chicago bluesman Earl Hooker, who always had the latest gear in town.

the danelectro sound

The key to a Danelectro's sound lies in the design of pickups: a single-coil design with wire wrapped around a straight bar magnet, encased in surplus chromed lipstick tubes, hence the nickname "lipstick tube pickups." The volume and tone controls comprised innovative stacked double pots, plus a pickup selector switch wired to give both pickups in series in the middle position. The series wiring gave a surprisingly strong tone, while the unique construction—a poplar neck with an aluminum nut, and a body frame made of light, inexpensive pine or poplar, capped back and front with painted sheets of ⅜ in. masonite—added to the Danelectro's honky, trebly tone.

below > **This bright red single-cutaway Danelectro U2 with its "coke bottle" headstock dates from 1958.**

right > **R. L. Burnside's stark, hypnotic rhythms echo the "fife and drum" band traditions of his isolated North Mississippi hill country home.**

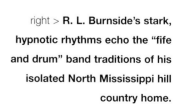

r. l. burnside

Like many bluesmen, contemporary North Mississippi hill country musician R. L. Burnside simply plays whatever comes along—maybe a Danelectro re-issue, or a Washburn, or a no-name Japanese guitar from the 1960s. These blues are bare-bones and immediate, typically a mesmeric, spiraling one-chord boogie with slashing bottleneck guitar that recalls his main influence, Mississippi Fred McDowell. No purist, Burnside's family band adds up-to-the-minute beats, bass and percussion, while his collaborations with the John Spencer Blues Explosion blurred the boundaries between blues and punk. "The blues started from how people was treated back in them slavery days," Burnside explains. "I keep on playing them so people can keep on remembering."

identifier

dating

1954–1955 Solid "peanut" bodies, no truss rods, aluminum bridge plates, some with aluminum frets.

1956–1957 Single-cutaway "U" models, truss rods, stainless steel bridge plates.

1958–1969 Double-cutaway "shorthorn" models. Also available in Deluxe trim, with "pointer" knobs, and in a semi-acoustic Convertible version.

1959–1969 "Longhorn" models.

serial numbers

Danelectros and Danelectro-made Silvertones usually carry their serial number inside the neck pocket. Numbers can be either three or four digits, and the last digit always indicates the last digit of the year. The first one or two digits correspond to the week of the year in which the guitar was built.

right > **In the late 1950s, fashion moved toward double cutaways. Double-cut Danelectros with the "seal"-shaped scratchplate were available from 1958 until the late 1960s.**

the guitar from mars
the fender stratocaster

Back in California, the Fender factory was getting even busier. By 1953, with the ultra-basic Telecaster picking up sales, Fender needed an upmarket model to incorporate all of Leo Fender's latest ideas. With steel guitarist and designer Freddie Tavares on board, Leo drew up not an upgrade for the Telecaster, but an all-new model, a guitar that would become perhaps the best all-round electric guitar of the twentieth century: the Stratocaster.

The fledgling Fender company relied upon feedback from a small number of respected local musicians. One of these was Bill Carson, a western swing player. Carson had test-driven the Telecaster and plenty of Fender amps; now he put his ideas for a new guitar to Leo, including a comfort-contoured body, multiple pickups, a new bridge with more individual string adjustment, a re-styled headstock like those found on custom guitars by the Californian inventor Paul Bigsby, and—most difficult of all—a vibrato that could bend the strings both up and down, and yet return accurately to pitch. It was a tall order, but Fender and Tavares set to work.

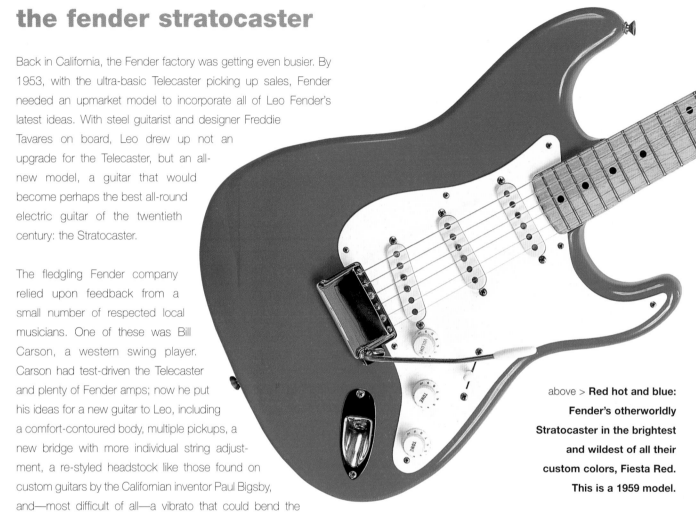

above > **Red hot and blue: Fender's otherworldly Stratocaster in the brightest and wildest of all their custom colors, Fiesta Red. This is a 1959 model.**

right > **The only known photograph of Guitar Slim, reputedly one of the all-time greatest blues showmen.**

"Guitar Slim was really something. I first saw him in Baton Rouge in 1954—he made his entrance from the back, sitting on the shoulders of a guy who must have weighed 300 pounds. I took the idea of using a 150-foot cord from him. He was also the first guy I saw using a Stratocaster. I was going 'What is that?'" **buddy guy**

guitar slim

Born plain Eddie Jones in Greenwood, Mississippi in 1926, Guitar Slim rose like a rocket to become New Orleans's most flamboyant blues star, yet he only scored one hit, "The Things I Used To Do," which ruled the R&B charts of 1954. Not only did Slim possess a great gospel voice, he also played spectacularly wild distorted lead guitar, dyed his hair to match his custom-made suits, and specialized in crowd-pleasing antics—like leading the entire audience out into the street and, via an extra-long guitar cable spooled out by an assistant, playing solos while duck-walking across a row of parked cars. Slim used Les Pauls, Telecasters, and Stratocasters, playing at mind-blowing volume through a PA amplifier; Earl King and Albert Collins worshiped his playing, as did the young Buddy Guy, who used to push his way to the front of many a show. "He could knock hell out of you with his guitar," recalls Buddy. "I think he was on drugs." Indeed, Guitar Slim led the kind of life that would kill most 1970s rock stars in a week. He died in 1959, aged just 32.

identifier

the first strats: 1954 to 1958

1954 Ash body, maple neck; finish: two-tone sunburst as standard, custom colors could be ordered; scratchplate: single layer white Bakelite, some with anodized aluminum. Approximate serial numbers: 0001–6999.

1955 Scratchplate: single layer white plastic. Optional fixed-bridge model introduced. Approximate serial numbers: 7000–8700.

1956 Hardware: gold plating optional. Approximate serial numbers: 9000–16000.

1957 Some examples with exaggerated v-shaped neck profile. Approximate serial numbers: 17000–24000.

1958 Last year for two-tone sunburst and the all-maple neck. Approximate serial numbers: 25000–30000.

below > **Fender's ads promoted a clean-cut, folksy image. Blues guitarists had other ideas.**

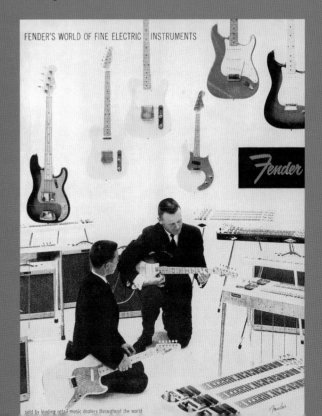

fender stratocaster
a revolution in sound

When the Stratocaster finally took shape it was still revolutionary. The sleek, sensual double-cutaway body featured comfort contours both back and front. There were three pickups arranged for maximum tonal variation, as on Gibson's ES-5 semi-acoustic, but with a slider switch allowing for split-second adjustments. There was a single master volume control for convenience, plus tone controls for the neck and middle pickups, and a stylish recessed jack socket.

Then there was the radical bridge system. This combined a tailpiece, an adjustable bridge, and a vibrato system all in one neat unit. Leo Fender and his team had considerable trouble with the design, and an expensive prototype was scrapped at a late stage (a much-modified version would eventually appear on the Jazzmaster in 1958). Eventually Fender hit upon a system whereby the bridgeplate pivoted on its front edge, while an array of adjustable springs in a rout in the rear of the body balanced the bridge against the pull of the strings.

In some quarters the space-age Stratocaster was met with disbelief, but for many blues players it was an instant hit. Ike Turner, Guitar Slim, Buddy Guy, and Pee Wee Crayton—a dazzling Texas-born guitarist who owned a rare early Strat, red with a gold anodized scratchplate—would all explore the outer limits of the Strat's potential long before Jimi Hendrix.

above > **The 1950s electric equivalent of Tampa Red's famous gold-plated National, this "gold on gold" 1957 Strat is finished in rare Shoreline Gold with custom-ordered gold-plated hardware.**

right > **Rhythm and blues power: the Ike & Tina Revue ripping it up in the 1960s. By this time Ike had moved on from a 1954 maple-neck Strat to a 1959 model in Sonic Blue with a slab rosewood fingerboard.**

identifier

ike turner

"I saw nobody but me playing a Stratocaster," Ike Turner claims. "I saw one in the window of a store in Memphis around 1954, and went straight in and bought it." Ike Turner, born 1931 in Clarksdale, MS, played piano on 1951's "Rocket 88," arguably the first-ever rock'n'roll record, and certainly one of the first songs with a fuzz guitar part (Willie Kizert's Fender Bassman amp had fallen from the trunk of the car onto the wet road, shorting one of the preamp tubes). Not only was Turner a gifted songwriter, a music business hustler, and leader of some of the hottest R&B shows of all time, including The Ike and Tina Turner Revue, he also played vicious, hyperactive Stratocaster lines with a unique vibrato-shuddering style. Turner contributed guitar on many Sun Records sessions, played with Howlin' Wolf and Elmore James, and it's him brilliantly torturing a Strat on some of Otis Rush's fabulous Cobra sides of the late 1950s.

custom colors

solid colors

in 1956 Fender began offering players the chance to own a Strat in shocking solid colors.

Up to the 1960s, when it introduced a proper "custom color" chart, Fender simply gave customers the opportunity to order a Strat in any color from the DuPont paint catalog for a mere 5 percent surcharge.

custom color

any custom color Fender from the 1950s is a rare collector's piece. The most-seen custom finishes include black, red, blue, gold, and white.

Many other colors are known to have been ordered, including Turquoise Metallic, Blond (standard on the Tele, but custom-order on the Strat: with gold hardware, these are known as "Mary Kaye" guitars after the well-known entertainer), Pink, and Blue Sparkle.

If you had paid that $25 color surcharge in 1954 and kept your guitar under the bed, it could now be worth $10,000 over a standard sunburst model—and maybe more.

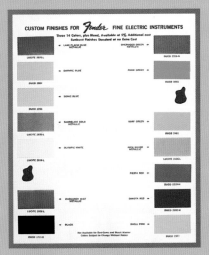

left > **To fly back to 1956 with $300 in your pocket ... Fender's custom-color chart.**

fender stratocaster
future blues

So familiar is the Fender Stratocaster today that it's hard to imagine the effect this uncompromisingly modern guitar—with its smooth, curved body and slick, curvaceous headstock—had on astounded onlookers in the 1950s. Even the vibrato seemed styled as much for effect as for function, with no visible springs, rollers or levers, just a silvery, wandlike control arm projecting magically from a neat, businesslike bridge.

Blues players had no qualms about embracing such a futuristic instrument. Jaw-dropping guitars had been a part of blues performance ever since the flashy pearl-inlaid flat-tops of the 1920s and the spectacular metal-bodied Nationals of the 1930s: getting noticed made you money. Plus, the Stratocaster was a real player's guitar. The vibrato offered a wider range of pitch-change than its main competitor, the Bigsby, while the positioning of the volume pot, tone pots, and the angled, sliding pickup selector switch allowed instant fingertip control over an undreamed-of range of sounds.

above right > **The first-ever "official" Fender Stratocaster custom color was a see-through blond not dissimilar to the standard Telecaster finish. Examples like this 1958 Strat with the gold hardware are known as "Mary Kaye models" after a well-known 1950s Fender endorsee.**

right > **Howlin' Wolf again, this time with a fine 1959 slab-board Strat.**

far right > **Buddy Guy, with his finger wrapped around the volume knob, tears it up on his much-missed 1957 sunburst Stratocaster.**

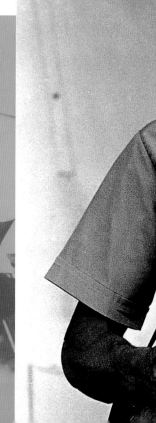

identifier

the strat conquers chicago

Magic Sam, a master of the soulful West Side sound, played some wonderful fingerpicked Stratocaster on a series of great Cobra singles from 1957, including his trademark "All Your Love." His reputation would be deservedly far higher today had he not died at the age of 32 in 1969.

A young Buddy Guy, inspired to play the electric guitar after witnessing Lightnin' Slim play—"It was like something exploding," he later marveled—bought his first Stratocaster for $179 in 1957, and used his Fender to forge a reputation as a true blues guitar showman with an uncanny ability to reproduce the styles of B. B. King, Magic Sam, Guitar Slim, and many more. "My original Strat was stolen," Guy mourns. "I knew who did it and tried to buy it back, but they were afraid of going to jail! I had the old Fender Bassman amp, too. Those two, the Strat and the Bassman, they go hand in hand."

vintage re-issues

Stung into action by the appearance of millimeter-perfect vintage Stratocaster copies by Japanese companies such as Tokai, Fender decided to market its own brand-new versions of vintage-specification guitars. Realizing that players didn't want re-invented Stratocasters, but guitars made the way they were in the 1950s and 1960s, the Vintage Re-issue range was launched in 1982. It contained two Stratocasters, not exact replicas but better in quality and vibe than the heavy, lumpy Strats of the 1970s:

57 Vintage Re-issue A re-working of the original, with a narrow-headstock maple neck, and a two-tone sunburst ash body.

62 Vintage Re-issue Also carried old-style hardware throughout but employed a rosewood fingerboard, 1960s-style colors, and a three-ply scratchplate.

Before long, Fender also acquired a facility in Japan to make vintage-style Fenders at even lower prices. Labeled as Fenders or as Squires, these Far East-manufactured 57 and 62 Strats offered an excellent facsimile of the vintage experience for cost-conscious players. Eventually the range would also include a 1968 Hendrix-era Strat and a wide-headstock 1972 re-issue.

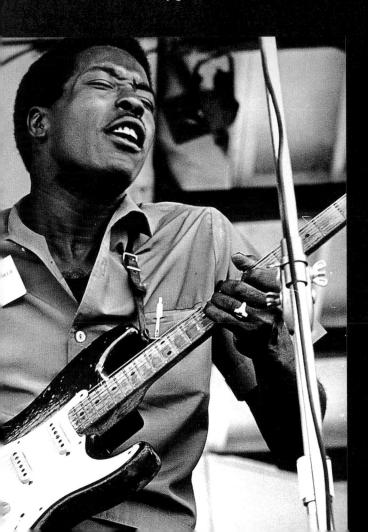

left > **The design may be 40 years old, but Fender's 1960s Strat re-issues still make good all-round budget working guitars. This is a modern Mexican model.**

the strat in the 1960s
back to the future

Instead of phasing out established models for new ones, Fender simply added new guitars to the line. The upmarket Jazzmaster, of 1958, never found much support in the blues world, perhaps thanks to its rather dark-sounding pickups—although Magic Slim bucked the trend when he emerged in the mid 1960s playing a Jazzmaster. Yet Fender was not above altering its designs to suit market forces, and it wasn't long after the birth of the Jazzmaster that it applied the new model's rosewood fingerboard across the entire range.

At first Fender glued a flat rosewood fingerboard to the necks of its Strats and Teles, but soon found a faster and cheaper method: by milling the surface of the neck blank to a curve, and gluing on a thin rosewood veneer. The new fingerboard made a subtle difference to the guitars' tone and feel, and even today some players choose the original maple-fingerboard's slick feel and snappy response, while others prefer the later guitars' rosewood fingerboards for their slightly sweeter tone. Ireland's beloved blues-rocker Rory Gallagher chose a 1961 Strat with a slab rosewood fingerboard—recently re-issued by Fender in a very limited edition, right down to the distressed finish.

above > **Though Fender was sold in 1965, the company could still make some stunning guitars. This 1966 Lake Placid Blue Strat has the new, wider headstock with a "transition" Fender logo.**

right > **Beloved Irish blues rocker Rory Gallagher with his battered 1960s Strat.**

far right > **Chicago's great left-hander, Otis Rush.**

identifier

robert cray

Robert Cray's tasteful, minimalist guitar style, his soulful, Memphis-tinged arrangements and his deceptively dark lyrics are pure class. Born in Georgia in 1953, Cray formed his first band in 1974 and was soon playing backup for his hero, the Texas Telecaster master Albert Collins. He hit the big time with 1983s *Bad Influence* and since then has reliably produced fine soul-meets-blues records that never stoop to the level of over-emotive blues-rock. An ambassador for the Strat for the past 20 years, Robert Cray's favorite guitar is a 1964 model he bought in 1969, with a non-vibrato bridge and an added top boost switch. These days he also plays various Fender Robert Cray models, custom-built by Fender with a combination of features from his 1964 and from a maple-neck 1958. His amps are 4 x 10-in. Fender Super Reverbs, sometimes augmented by 2 x 12-in. Twin Reverbs.

strats in the 1960s

1959 Strat fingerboard changes from maple to a "slab" of rosewood. Standard sunburst finish becomes three-tone, with added red. Scratchplate changes from white to three-layer greenish-tinted white/black/white, with 11 screws. Custom colors become a standard range: Fiesta Red, Shoreline Gold, Olympic White, Desert Sand, Dakota Red, Lake Placid Blue. Serial numbers (approximate): 30000–40000.

1960 New custom colors include Daphne Blue, Shell Pink, Candy Apple Red, Inca Silver, Burgundy Mist, Sonic Blue, Foam Green and Surf Green. Serial numbers: 40000–50000.

1961 Serial numbers: 50000–70000.

1962 Slab fingerboard dropped for veneered type. Serial numbers: 60000–90000.

1963 Serial numbers: 80000–90000 and L10000–L20000.

1964 Serial numbers: L20000–L50000.

1965 Fingerboard dot markers change from "clay" to pearl. The Columbia Broadcasting Corporation buy Fender for $13,000,000—the end of the "pre-CBS" era. Serial numbers: L50000–L90000 and some 100000s.

1966 New, larger peghead. The maple-necked Strat is re-introduced as an option, but with a separate fingerboard. Serial numbers: 100000–200000.

left > **Robert Cray often uses sweet, pingy "out of phase" tones—a sound made much easier to achieve after five-way switches were introduced in the 1970s.**

stevie ray vaughan

supercharging the blues

There's one simple reason for the Fender Stratocaster's current pre-eminence in modern electric blues: Stevie Ray Vaughan. Stevie Ray's slamming guitar style was the shot in the arm the blues needed. When he died on August 27, 1990, in a post-show helicopter crash that also claimed three of Eric Clapton's entourage, it was a blow from which the music world has never really recovered.

Stevie grew up in Dallas' Oak Cliffs surrounded by his brother Jimmie's record collection: Buddy Guy, Eric Clapton, Muddy Waters, Albert Collins, and Guitar Slim. But Stevie had three main influences: the tough, uncompromising Albert King, Howlin' Wolf's guitarist Hubert Sumlin, and Memphis guitar slinger Lonnie Mack.

the new texas blues sound

Vaughan was a Strat man through and through. His main guitar was his beloved "Number One"—a 1962 Stratocaster whose sunburst finish carried the scars of its owner's ferocious pick attack, purchased in the mid 1970s and played right up until the night he died. Number One was fitted with a wide "D profile" neck with a rosewood-veneer fingerboard and heavy-gauge jumbo frets, and it carried a set of specially hot 1959 pickups that Fender itself would use as the basis for its Texas Special units. In the early 1980s Vaughan swapped the original white scratchplate for a black one carrying his initials in truck-stop stick-on decals, and also added a left-handed tremolo block.

Even though Vaughan used notoriously heavy strings—generally 0.013 in. to 0.058 in., and occasionally a 0.15 in. on the top—string-breakage was still an ever-present problem, and so each string carried a short strip of electrical wire sleeving at the point that it passed over the bridge. Eventually the guitar received new gold-plated hardware, and the original neck was retired as the fingerboard had simply been worn too thin to be re-fretted any more. After Vaughan's death the original neck and body were reunited, and the guitar is now in the possession of his brother. SRV's other Strats included Red, another 1962 model that was fitted with various necks, both modern and

above and right > **Chief of the new rock blues revival Stevie Ray Vaughan, pictured above with his favorite "Number One" Strat and, right, with Lenny, a maple-neck custom with his trademark truck-stop stickers.**

vintage reproduction; Lenny, a brown-stained guitar with an inlaid butterfly that was a gift from Stevie's then wife, Leonora; Butter, a stock 1961 that Vaughan appropriated when he discovered it being given away by some concert promoters; and Charley, a pearlescent white mongrel fitted with a hardtail bridge and three original Danelectro "lipstick tube" pickups.

Amps were just as much a part of Vaughan's legendary tone as his guitars. As a young Dallas hotshot he used various pairs of Fenders, changing as breakdowns and finances allowed between 40-watt 4 x 10-in. Super Reverbs, 40-watt 2 x 10-in. Vibroverbs and 2 x 12 in. Twin Reverbs. Occasionally he would choose a Marshall Town & Country combo, and later would augment his preferred Super Reverbs with a Dumble 150 Steel String Singer or 200-watt Marshall Majors. He also employed a Fender Vibratone rotating-speaker cabinet and in the studio occasionally chose a Fender Harvard and a 1959 Bassman. His effects included Ibanez Tube Screamers, an old 1960s Vox wah, a modified Dallas-Arbiter Fuzz Face and a Tycobrahe Octavia.

guitars of the stars
fender's name game

By the late 1980s, the Stratocaster had established itself as the most popular electric guitar on the market—a real all-rounder, capable of covering everything from rock to soul. It had also cemented a reputation as the best all-round electric for the blues, with a vast following including names like Ronnie Earl, Duke Robillard, Jimmie Vaughan, and Kenny Wayne Shepherd. At the same time, and with a degree of irony, the blues began to mean something in marketing terms. Suddenly vintage blues and soul music were being employed to represent passion, originality, and an all-American authenticity—qualities that manufacturers of everything from jeans to guitars were only too eager to see reflected back onto their products. After years of ignoring players from the wrong side of the tracks, the music industry would soon come to realize that blues players could be valuable endorsees.

above > **Texas style: this popular signature model Strat is an off-the-peg solution for players who want to wear their Stevie Ray Vaughan influence around their neck.**

Fender quickly took the opportunity to strengthen its image with a range of new guitars that reflected the specifications of blues stars' personal instruments. The Eric Clapton Stratocaster, launched in 1988, combined high-tech Lace Sensor pickups, a rocking mid-boost feature, and a vintage 1930s Martin-inspired neck profile, to great acclaim. The 1992 Stevie Ray Vaughan signature model recreated Stevie's famous Number One guitar, with re-voiced pickups, a left-handed vibrato, and an engraved scratchplate—everything, in fact, apart from the wear and tear of several thousand nights' playing. Ask Fender's custom shop nicely, though, and it can fix that as well.

right > **Bonnie Raitt's personalized guitar, a 1970s-flavored Strat with a narrow neck, is an excellent and underrated all-rounder.**

eric clapton and blackie

Through the 1970s Eric Clapton's main guitar was his famous black Stratocaster, "Blackie." Blackie was in fact constructed by Clapton himself from an assortment of 1950s and 1960s parts. Visiting Nashville he had come across the Sho-Bud pedal steel store, which had a number of then-unfashionable vintage Strats for a few hundred dollars apiece. Clapton bought several and carried them home to England, handing out one to Steve Winwood, one to Pete Townshend and one to George Harrison as gifts. From the remainder Clapton built himself one guitar with his favorite body, the best neck and the best-sounding pickups. This was the guitar that Fender used in 1988 as the basis for its first-ever signature guitar, the Clapton Strat.

below > **Eric Clapton with his trademark black Fender, the guitar that inspired 1988s Clapton Strat, plus mid-boost and a notably fine-feeling neck.**

identifier

fender's blues stratocasters

stevie ray vaughan Fender's posthumous SRV tribute guitar carries a pau ferro fingerboard, Stevie's favorite oval neck shape, Texas Special pickups, gold hardware, a left-handed vibrato, and an engraved pickguard.

robert cray The Robert Cray Stratocaster has custom-wound pickups, a 1960s-style rosewood fingerboard, and a fixed non-vibrato bridge.

bonnie raitt The slide star's personal Strat model marries 1960s and 1970s specifications, including an alder body, Texas Special pickups, a wide 1970s-style headstock and a special narrow "C" shaped neck.

jimmie vaughan This laudably affordable blues-oriented Stratocaster, made in Mexico, features a "V"-shaped neck, three Fender Tex-Mex pickups with a specially hot bridge unit, and custom wiring that leaves the middle pickup "wide open."

buddy guy Buddy Guy's signature model comes in a 1950s style two-tone sunburst or in black with extrovert polka dots. The neck has a V-shaped profile, while the pickups are Gold Fender-Lace Sensors.

below > **Buddy Guy with his polka-dot signature Strat.**

fender stratocaster

the southern slide sound

None of the classic guitar designs of the twentieth century were intended for playing blues. Traditionally, Gibson sought the approval of respected jazz players. In California, Fender loaned its prototype guitars to Western Swing guitarists. Gibson would have been extremely surprised to see what its instruments were capable of when plugged into a loud, filthy-sounding amp, and somehow the Stratocaster has emerged as a pre-eminent electric for slide playing, especially for Texas blues.

On one hand the Strat's extreme fingerboard radius makes it an unlikely partner for the application of a short, straight chunk of metal tubing. In reality Leo Fender developed his earliest pickups specifically for lap-steels, so he knew all about precise pickup placement and the voicing of sweet-sounding single-coils. Today, the extraordinary Louisiana blues and zydeco slide player Sonny Landreth plays Strats, while rootsy bottleneck ambassador Ry Cooder has long employed a Fender—although his has been converted with a Japanese Teisco lap-steel pickup. When not playing acoustic, John Lee Hooker's one-time sideman Roy Rogers also uses a Strat. Maybe the mark of a truly great guitar lies in its ability to transcend its intended parameters.

above > **Though 1970s Strats display "undesirable" features— "bullet" truss rods, three-bolt necks, and thick, glossy lacquer—Little Feat's slide master Lowell George didn't let it bother him. This guitar dates from 1973.**

right > **Sonny Landreth's startling bottleneck sound is partly based on his technique of fretting notes "behind" the slide. As well as American Standard Strats with multi-tuning Hipshot Trilogy mechanisms, he has used a vintage Gibson Firebird, a Gibson Melody Maker, a steel-bodied James Trussart electric, and a 1970s Dobro.**

identifier

bonnie raitt

Queen of the slide-driven Stratocaster, Bonnie Raitt was born in Burbank, California in 1949, but attended college in Cambridge, Massachusetts, where she grabbed the opportunity to learn guitar first-hand from bottle-neck pioneers Son House and Mississippi Fred McDowell. Her first album enlisted the help of harpist Junior Wells and blues sax player A. C. Reed, and, though her subsequent records have delved into rock and pop, Raitt is still a hugely accomplished and instantly recognizable slide stylist with a sweet, singing tone. After a period of personal problems brought on by living and partying just as hard as her blues heroes, Raitt made a spectacular return with 1989's *Nick Of Time*, appeared in fine form as a guest on John Lee Hooker's all-star *The Healer* album of 1990, and since then has cemented her reputation as one of the first women of the blues.

below > **Bonnie Raitt with her treasured Stratocaster, "Brown"—bought in 1969 for $120.**

strats in the 1970s

from 1965 Fender's new owners CBS did little to alter the basic design of the Stratocaster and the model continued to enjoy great success—indeed, after the appearance of Jimi Hendrix, sales went through the roof. But some small things changed, and players also began to notice a decline in quality and finesse, with heavier bodies and thicker neck lacquer.

first changes One of CBS's first changes was to enlarge the headstock and to add a more prominent logo.

around 1971 CBS abandoned the original four-bolt neck-fixing system and substituted a three-bolt version with a little-used Micro-Tilt neck adjuster, and shifted the truss rod adjusting bolt from the body end of the neck to the headstock, where it was topped with an ugly "bullet" nut.

early 1970s Pickup changes also arrived in the early 1970s, with flat polepieces replacing the traditional staggered variety, while the white pickguard swapped to black.

below > **Ry Cooder has a penchant for fitting his Strats with old Japanese lap steel pickups.**

gibson es-335 pure tone

Claiming the crown as probably the finest blues electric of all time, Gibson's ES-335, with every single element working in harmony, was a perfect cross between a solid electric and a true jazz guitar. Launched in 1958, the 335 was an all-laminated semi-acoustic, slimmer, and more comfortable than any before ("the wonder-thin silhouette," boasted Gibson), with a radical double-cutaway body that allowed access to the highest reaches of the 22-fret neck. The design was without doubt the crowning achievement of Gibson's Ted McCarty. Though the Les Paul solidbody is more famous, it's inextricably linked with Les Paul himself—who still claims the lion's share of the credit. The 335 was a 100 percent Gibson effort, and though the Stratocaster may have been in the back of their minds when they drew up the double-cutaway shape, McCarty said it was because he'd noticed that some players were beginning to use their thumbs to fret the sixth string. Weight was also a factor. Though the Les Paul was compact, it was an extremely heavy guitar. The 335 was considerably lighter, and the wide yet shallow body gained it the reputation of being the most wearable guitar on the market.

The 335 came fitted with Gibson's new, rich-sounding humbuckers, and was constructed with an innovative solid maple center block, virtually removing all unwanted feedback. This design also abandoned the traditional trapeze tailpiece in favor of a Les Paul-style Tune-O-Matic bridge and stop tailpiece for maximum sustain—the real key to the 335's incomparable sound.

The resulting power and sensitivity has made the 335 an all-round winner; from the cleanest of jazz to the dirtiest rock'n'roll, and the guitar and its close relations have earned a staggering user list: rockers like Ritchie Blackmore and Alvin Lee, jazz players from Larry Carlton and Lee Ritenour to John Scofield, and a whole host of the best blues talent including B. B. King, Freddie King, Mick Taylor, and Elvin Bishop. Eric Clapton still has the red 1964 he played with Cream, plus a rare 1959 blond dot-neck and a sunburst dot-neck from 1960.

above > **Solid gold classic: A dot-neck Gibson ES-335TDN from 1959. "T" stands for "thinline," "D" for "double pickups," and "N" for "natural."**

johnny "guitar" watson

One of the most outrageous guitarists on the West Coast scene, if not of all time, Johnny "Guitar" Watson, born in 1935 in Houston, Texas, moved to LA at the age of 15. In 1954 he cut the staggering guitar instrumental "Space Guitar"—a hyper-speed fingerpicked tour de force that in terms of both sound and technique was at least a decade ahead of its time. After cutting a number of great blues-steeped tunes in the 1950s, including the original "Gangster Of Love," he veered sidewise into jazz and then re-emerged in the 1970s as a purveyor of wicked old-school funk. Watson used a number of different types of guitars during his career: he was an early Strat exponent, and later employed various Gibson thinline semis and a Gibson SG Standard, but his sound was always utterly distinctive—and always pure blues. Johnny "Guitar" Watson passed away in 1996 on the verge of yet another spectacular comeback.

identifier

335 timeline

1958 The 335 is introduced with a 16 in. wide, 1 ⅝ in. deep body, two PAF humbuckers, and a stop tailpiece and Tune-O-Matic bridge. Finishes comprised sunburst and natural blond (the most sought-after vintage 335).

1959 Cherry finish is introduced.

1960 "Long" pickguard extending below the bridge changed for shorter type.

1962 "Block" fingerboard markers replace the original dots, and extra-rounded body horns are subtly slimmed down.

1964 The stop tailpiece, the heart of the 335 design, is dropped and replaced with a normal semi-acoustic trapeze tailpiece.

1970 A strengthening volute is added to the neck behind the nut.

1982 Gibson's first-ever true re-issue, the 335 Dot, is introduced.

right > **The 335 has remained in production ever since 1958. This modern cherry red version comes with Gibson's 1957 Classic pickups.**

gibson es-345 stereo blues

Inspired by the instant success of the ES-335, Gibson began to expand the range upward and offer a little more decoration. The ES-345 of 1959 followed the same magic formula—a mahogany neck with a laminated maple body, two humbuckers and a stop tailpiece screwed straight through to the center block—but added flash came courtesy of a pearl crown headstock inlay, gold-plated hardware, and double-parallelogram fingerboard inlays borrowed from the ES-175 jazz guitar.

Gibson promised that this new model would give "any sound you've ever heard from any guitar." The heart of the new electronics system was the Vari-tone selector, a six-position rotary switch that fed the output from the pickups through an assortment of capacitors, progressively reducing the rich hallmark Gibson tone to something approximating the sound of a single-coil guitar. Most players, in truth, chose to leave the Vari-tone in the bypass position. More scope was provided by two output jacks. These allowed the player to feed each pickup into a different amplifier for more volume and tonal variation, although buying a "Y cord"—a lead with one jack at one end and two at the other—meant that both pickups could still be fed into a single amplifier if required. Chicago stalwart Little Milton played a 1959 ES-345 through Acoustic amplifiers, while the young Robert Cray and Australian bluesman Dave Hole have also played ES-345s.

above > **Blues players loved the extra-rich look of the ES-345 with its gold hardware and fancy neck inlays. This desirable blond version dates from 1959.**

"I got into Fenders after seeing Earl Hooker, but then I ran into a Gibson guitar, and I liked that too. It's a warmer sound." otis rush

otis rush

A master of the soulful Chicago West Side sound, Otis Rush, born in 1934 in Philadelphia, Mississippi, grew up listening to John Lee Hooker and Howlin' Wolf. Visiting Chicago, he ran into a show by Muddy Waters. "Muddy, Jimmy Rogers on guitar, Junior Wells on harp—it was some band," Rush comments. "I said, this is for me!" After intense practice, Rush formed his own band and recorded a handful of astonishingly emotive songs for Cobra records, including "Double Trouble," "I Can't Quit You Baby," and "Groaning The Blues," showcasing the vicious Strat playing of Ike Turner and Rush's almost vocal vibrato, played upside down on a right-handed guitar. Alas, his 1960s work with Chess and Vanguard saw few sales, but 1994's *Ain't Enough Comin' In* was a big return to form and 1998's *Any Place I'm Going* won a well-deserved Grammy. Rush swaps between a custom 1962-style Strat, a red right-handed ES-345, and a left-handed 1962 ES-355.

identifier

es-345 timeline

1959 ES-345TD introduced with split parallelogram fingerboard inlays and gold-plated tuners, Tune-O-Matic bridge, stop tailpiece, and pickups. A Vari-tone rotary control with stereo electronics that fed the output of each pickup to a separate jack. Finishes included sunburst and the rare natural blond, available 1959 only.

1960 Cherry finish optional. Pickguard altered from "long" to "short" type. Vari-tone selector gains gold surround.

1964 Stop tailpiece abandoned for gold-plated trapeze tailpiece.

1959 Walnut finish available.

1982 Stop tailpiece re-introduced, but model dropped in same year. Gibson introduced a re-issue ES-345 in 2002.

es-347 Gibson's replacement for the ES-345 and ES-355 was a new model that kept some upmarket features but dropped the Vari-tone in place of a more modern coil-tap switch, and added a fine-tuning TP6 tailpiece and hot Dirty Fingers humbuckers. Introduced in 1978, the ES-347 is still in production.

right > **A cherry red ES-345 from 1963. This particular guitar was probably retro-fitted with a Bigsby vibrato at the factory: The "Custom Made" plaque covers the holes for the original stop tailpiece.**

gibson es-355 king of the thinlines

The top model in Gibson's new thin-bodied, semi-solid guitar line was the fabulous ES-355. Like the ES-345, the 355 carried a Vari-tone selector and stereo wiring—although the very first examples were mono, and mono was available throughout the 1960s as an option. The company heaped on some extra trimmings, including extra body binding, a split-diamond pearl headstock inlay, pearl block markers in place of double parallelograms on an ebony fingerboard, and a vibrato as standard.

The ES-355 proved reasonably popular, with a strong appreciation among blues and R&B players from Jimmy Rogers to Chuck Berry, but despite Gibson's best efforts it sold more of the workmanlike ES-335s than glamorous ES-345s and ES-355s. The shipping totals tell the story: for 1960 the respective figures were 514 for the 335, 521 for the 345 and 317 for the 355; by 1962 the respective numbers

were 876, 306 and 220—and by 1967, when thinline guitar production peaked, Gibson was making nearly six thousand 335s per year but only eleven hundred 345s and just four hundred 355s. Today, it's the basic 335 that fetches the highest prices—and the rare early blond examples are among the most sought-after electric guitars of the all.

above > **Pure glamor: a 1959 355 with all the trimmings including gold hardware, block inlays, multiple binding, and a tortoiseshell pickguard. As few players used the Vari-tone and stereo options, Gibson soon introduced a simpler mono model that proved more popular.**

left > **Rock'n'roll pioneer Chuck Berry has a canny attitude toward buying guitars—and cars: he purchases a new one each year, storing the old ones away as investments.**

identifier

jimmy rogers

The engine room of the early 1950s Muddy Waters band, Jimmy Rogers—born James Lane in Ruleville, Mississippi, in 1924—typified the Chicago rhythm guitar sound, with muscular bass lines, spare, well-timed single-note fills, and chord work that intertwined instinctively with Otis Spann's piano and Waters' slide guitar. He was an excellent writer, too, penning songs like "Ludella," "That's All Right," "Sloppy Drunk," and "Walking By Myself." Rogers had arrived in Chicago in the early 1940s, and was soon acting as sideman for Sunnyland Slim, Tampa Red, and Memphis Minnie, playing Big Bill Broonzy-style on a flat-top acoustic with a DeArmond jammed in the soundhole. Later he would choose a Silvertone, a 1970s Gibson Super 400, and an Epiphone Rivera, but his best-known guitar was a black Gibson 355. After Waters arrived on the scene in 1947, the pair hooked up with harp player Little Walter, and Chicago's best and most important band was born. Rogers quit in the mid 1950s to be replaced by Pat Hare, and spent much of the 1960s running a clothing business. Coming out of retirement after the store was burned down in the riots that followed the death of Martin Luther King, he made several impressive returns to the recording studio before his death in 1997.

right > **The underrated Jimmy Rogers was part of Muddy Waters' awe-inspiring band of the early 1950s. They earned the nickname "The Headhunters" for their habit of "cutting the heads" of any other act with whom they shared a stage.**

355 timeline

1959 The first mono ES-355TD comes onto the market with a Bigsby vibrato as standard, a multiple-bound body and neck, block markers on an ebony fingerboard, and a five-piece "split diamond" pearl headstock inlay. Cherry is the only finish available. The ES-355TDSV, introduced in late 1959, carried a Vari-tone and stereo circuitry.

1961 A side-to-side action vibrato replaces the Bigsby.

1962 Grover Rotomatic tuners change to Klusons.

1963 More vibrato changes: the latest Gibson version carries a lyre-engraved coverplate.

1967 Tuners revert to Grovers.

1969 Walnut finish option introduced, and the Bigsby returns.

1970 Mono ES-355TD discontinued.

1978 Bigsbys are dropped—again—and the Gibson vibrato makes a comeback.

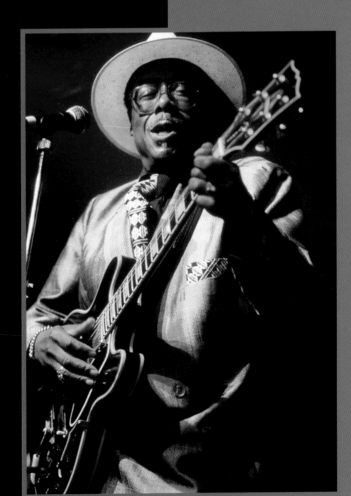

b. b. king

the undisputed truth

Riley "Blues Boy" King is the acknowledged master of postwar electric blues. It's impossible to overstate this genial maestro's contribution to the genre. Over the last half century B. B. King has been one of the blues' greatest bandleaders, most soulful vocalists, and most gifted interpreters. He's also an utterly distinctive guitar stylist with a unique fingertip vibrato and immaculate phrasing—a jazz lover at heart, but a true bluesman who can cram more soul into a micro-tone bend than you'd imagine possible.

Born in Itta Bena, Mississippi, in 1925, Riley King sang gospel in church but discovered that the blues worked better on the street. His main guitar influences included the jazzy side of blues—T-Bone Walker and Lonnie Johnson—and jazz itself, including Charlie Christian and Django Reinhardt. In 1948 he spent some ten months in Memphis learning guitar from his uncle, slide player Bukka White, and soon returned there to claim his own show on radio WDIA, one of the first truly black music friendly stations.

Two years after first entering a recording studio King scored his first chart placing with 1951's "Three O'Clock Blues," and since then he has enjoyed success in every decade. The 1950s produced "You Know I Love You," "Every Day I Have The Blues," and almost 20 others. The 1960s bore "Sweet Sixteen," "How Blue Can You Get," "Payin' The Cost To Be The boss," the remarkable *Live At The Apollo album*, and a huge mainstream crossover hit in "The Thrill Is Gone." In the 1970s he adopted the smooth Philly sound to great acclaim, while the 1980s and 1990s spawned some fine guest-album LPs like *Blues Summit*—and in case anyone thinks that King has forgotten his roots, try *Let The Good Times Roll*, a fine recent collection of Louis Jordan jump-blues classics. B. B. King has played probably in excess of 15,000 concerts, has recorded with everyone from Duke Ellington to U2, and is, without doubt, King Of The Blues.

the king and lucille

Pictures from the late 1940s show B. B. King playing a basic Gibson ES-125, a simple noncutaway archtop electric with a single P-90 pickup. By the 1950s he had moved on to try other guitars, first a Telecaster, then a Gretsch, then a Silvertone, then flashier, more expensive semi-acoustics like a short-scale, twin-pickup Gibson Byrdland, and a three-pickup Gibson ES-5. One night in the 1950s King was playing a show in a small town in Arkansas when two men fighting over a woman kicked over a kerosene stove, setting fire to the building. King ran inside to retrieve his guitar

and almost didn't make it back alive. The woman, he learned, was named Lucille, and since then he has named every one of his guitars after her to remind himself not to be so foolish again.

Around 1959 B. B. King discovered Gibson's ES-355 and never looked back: "It was like finding your wife," he said. Ever since 1980 he has played a Gibson B. B. King Lucille model, a luxury 355 with no f-holes. Tube amplifier addicts might like to note that B. B. King uses a solid-state Gibson Lab Series amp from the 1970s.

above > **A tribute to the master: Gibson's sealed-body B. B. King "Lucille" model. King keeps his Vari-tone control in the center position with both pickups permanently on, and constantly adjusts his sound via the volume pots.**

gibson es-330 blues on a budget

The Les Paul and the ES-335 might be the cornerstones of Gibson's electric guitar legacy, but humbler models like the ES-330 were the company's biggest sellers in the first half of the 1960s. Howlin' Wolf played an ES-330 around this time, and Blue Note recording star Grant Green used one to great effect on his bestselling jazz instrumental albums. Today, blues players such as Rusty Zinn have rediscovered the ES-330's unique qualities.

The ES-330's pickups are nonadjustable single-coil P-90s, the short neck joins restrict access to the upper frets, and the body is entirely hollow. Because of this, the ES-330 gained a reputation of being impossible to play at high volume without feedback problems. However, players are now rejecting the super-loud 100-watt stacks of the 1970s in favor of smaller, lower-powered amps, with improved PA technology taking over the task of delivering the sound of the whole band. These days the ES-330 is regarded as a minor jazz/blues classic—and vintage models are available for a fraction of the price of a 1959 ES-335.

above right > **It might look much like a 335, but the hollow body and twin P-90s places the ES-330 in the same family as Gibson's ES-125TD and ES-225TD. Examples like this from 1961 or 1962 sometimes combine the early-type dot markers with the later nickel pickup covers.**

right > ***Tip On In*** **made the R&B charts in 1967, and the sleeve shows Slim Harpo complete with his faithful ES-330, Fender amp, and harmonica rack.**

slim harpo

One of the ES-330's most faithful users was bluesman Slim Harpo, born James Moore in Lobdell, Louisiana in 1924. Moore first took the name Harmonica Slim, playing electric guitar and a harmonica in a rack, with a laid-back, easy-rocking style that borrowed from his great hero, Jimmy Reed. He changed his name to Slim Harpo in the mid 1950s and scored his first hit, "I'm A King Bee," backed with "Got Love If You Want It," in 1957. Harpo's great skill was in delivering danceable Saturday night blues that blurred the boundary between down home blues and pop accessibility. His repertoire proved a goldmine for 1960s white R&B acts like The Rolling Stones, The Yardbirds, Them, The Kinks, and even David Bowie. Harpo enjoyed great success by teaming up with his old friend Lightning Slim to play for rock audiences, but he died of a heart attack on the eve of a European tour in 1970. His songs are played by the likes of Lou Ann Barton, John Hammond, and The Fabulous Thunderbirds, and Slim Harpo's swampy, good-time blues still sound great today.

identifier

es-330 timeline

the es-330's lack of labels and serial numbers means dating is best done by a combination of features and the factory order number.

1959 ES-330TD ("Thin Double") twin pickup and ES-330T ("Thin") single pickup models introduced. Double rounded cutaway slimline body with no center block. Neck joins the body at the 16th fret. Tune-O-Matic bridge with trapeze tailpiece: Bigsby vibrato only rarely appears as a factory option—most will have been added later. Black-covered P-90 pickups, white-bound fingerboard with pearl "dot" markers. Finishes: sunburst and the rarer blond.

1962 Cherry finish available. "Dot" fingerboard markers change to small pearl blocks. Shape of body changes slightly, with the extra-rounded horns becoming slimmer. Black plastic pickup covers change to metal.

1963 Single-pickup ES-330T discontinued.

1967–1969 Burgundy Sparkle finish available.

1969 Neck lengthened to join the body at the 19th fret.

1972 Model discontinued.

The ES-330TD is now once again available from Gibson as a re-issue.

right > **The Epiphone Casino of 1961–1970 was essentially an ES-330 with slight cosmetic changes.**

epiphone the master built guitar

Gibson may have ruled the archtop guitar market, but by the 1930s it had stiff competition from Epiphone and its superb "Masterbilt" guitars. Epiphone started out making banjos in the 1920s, but after the stock market crash of 1929 it successfully edged away from the fast-declining banjo market with a line of innovative flat-top acoustics. Epiphone's Emperor guitar of 1935 made a bid for the throne occupied by Gibson's spectacular Super 400 jazz guitar, and followed up strongly with an electric archtop in 1937, and a wide range of medium-priced acoustic archtops.

But with the death of company founder Epaminodas Stathopoulo in the early 1940s, Epiphone lost its stomach for the fight. Quality suffered, sales dived, and in 1957 Gibson bought out its once-feared rival for the bargain sum of $20,000—not just the name, but the entire stock of parts and manufacturing equipment. Gibson swiftly set about annihilating the old models and re-establishing Epiphone as a line of "almost-Gibson" guitars, specifically aimed at the many music stores who had been waiting in vain for a coveted Gibson dealership.

above right > **This glorious Gibson-made Epiphone Sheraton from 1961 combined traditional Epiphone features—the "V-block" neck inlays and the "vine" headstock decoration— with the slimline 335 design.**

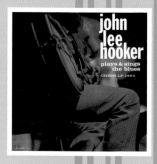

right > **Recorded in a single day in 1965, *The Real Folk Blues* was a fully-electric album that showed Hooker at his best, stretching and twisting a selection of originals and heavily re-worked covers into a compelling whole. It included one of his best-known songs, "One Bourbon, One Scotch, One Beer," an adaptation of a classic Amos Milburn drinking tune.**

identifier

john lee hooker

John Lee Hooker had the Midas touch in reverse: everything he played turned into the deep, dark soil of his Clarksdale, Mississippi birthplace. Hooker's blues is a conundrum: hip and urbane, yet utterly down-home. Around the clubs of 1950s Chicago and Detroit his style was regarded as a Delta blues throw-back, and indeed Hooker owed his spooky, ringing guitar sound to his stepfather, Will Moore. He received his first guitar from T-Bone Walker and began recording in the late 1940s, with a lone guitar and a piece of plywood to stamp his feet upon. "Boogie Chillen" (1948), a hypnotic single-chord modal drone with primal ahead-of-the-beat accents, sold a million copies in a single year. Later Chicago sessions added harmonica, electric guitar, and drums; in the 1960s Hooker stripped his sound back to more relaxed folk-blues and also experimented with rock backing, notably with Canned Heat. In the 1980s, with the aid of tough management and polished PR, Hooker hauled himself out of a creative quagmire with a string of hugely popular guest-artist albums—*The Healer, Mr Lucky, Boom Boom, Chill Out*—which established him as the world's greatest purveyor of good-time spiritual boogie.

Aside from Old Blondie, his 1950s Epiphone Broadway, pictured below, John Lee Hooker favored Gibson ES-335s and Epiphone Sheraton thinline semi-acoustics, Epiphone's equivalent to the ES-355.

epiphone's thinlines

the sheraton was the top model, with a pearl "vine" headstock inlay, two mini-humbucking pickups, luxury touches like multiple binding and "V-block" fingerboard inlays and Epiphone's distinctive two-piece Frequensator trapeze tailpiece. The Sheraton came in sunburst, natural, or cherry and was made from 1958 until 1970. Soon afterward, Epiphone production was moved to the Far East.

the rivera was designed to echo the "basic" ES-335, with simpler binding and fingerboard inlays and nickel hardware.

the casino, the cheapest of Epiphone's thinline semis, was a fully hollow guitar with one or two single-coil P90 pickups. Effectively a Gibson ES-330 but with an Epiphone headstock and a slightly slimmer neck, the Casino found fame in the hands of John Lennon and Paul McCartney.

above right > **Modern Sheratons and Riveras are once again being made in the USA.**
right > **This Sheraton is fitted with Epiphone's Frequensator tailpiece, a design intended to give optimum tension for the bass and treble strings.**

epiphone rise and fall

Epiphone's demise in the 1950s was a sad end to a great line of guitars. Part of the reason that quality fell so much was that when production shifted from New York to Philadelphia in 1953, some of the company's most skilled workers jumped ship to the new Guild factory—and many early Guild archtops bear a strong resemblance to Epiphones.

During the 1960s, however, Gibson did preserve the Epiphone reputation. It retained the beautiful triple-pickup single-cutaway thinline Emperor, and generated a new line of interesting solid-bodies including the Crestwood and Wilshire—which despite their SG-like all-mahogany construction aped Fender styling in a way Gibson could never be seen to do—and the Coronet, a light, powerful, no-frills alternative to the Les Paul Junior. Gibson's own financial troubles of the 1970s and 1980s meant that Epiphone manufacture was steadily downgraded from Japan to Korea, but recently Gibson have started up US production for various classic models, including the Casino and even a John Lee Hooker signature model.

above > **The original Emperor was one of Epiphone's finest jazz guitars. By 1963, when this example was made, Gibson had abandoned the clunky push-button switching system and slimmed the body down to more comfortable proportions.**

above > **Precious Bryant.**

left > **Taj Mahal with an oval-soundhole Epiphone Howard Roberts.**

epiphone blues

Cedell Davis, born in Helena, Arkansas in 1927, is one of the most challenging hard-core bluesmen playing today, with a uniquely stark, almost atonal sound. Struck down with polio as a child, he was forced to re-learn the guitar left-handed; instead of fretting the strings normally he chose to play in an "overhand" slide style, using the handle of a table knife. From 1953 to 1963 Davis formed a partnership with Robert Nighthawk, one of the Delta's most respected slide players, even though he was confined to a wheelchair after being injured in a juke-joint stampede. His recent album *The Horror Of It All* (Fat Possum Records) is a reminder that completely unique forms of blues can still flourish today, just as they did before the Depression.

Another current Epiphone player is blueswoman Precious Bryant, born in 1942 in Talbot County, Georgia. Bryant sings the songs of Jimmy Reed, Muddy Waters, and Elmore James, and plays thumbpick-style on a 1960s Epiphone Howard Roberts, an oval-hole single-pickup jazz guitar. She is one of the last living links to the stylish, upbeat blues tradition of southwest Georgia.

below > **Cedell Davis, playing overhand style with a table knife.**

identifier

epiphone pickups

Epiphone's archtop guitars of the late 1930s and early 1940s came with "oblong" single coils with large slot-head polepieces. By 1950, two more versions arrived: a large metal-covered single-coil looking much like a later Gibson humbucker, with a single offset row of polepieces, and the "New York" pickup, a narrower type with white plastic ends and the polepieces arrayed along the very edge of the pickup cover. Neither one is greatly treasured by blues players today.

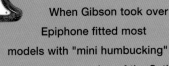

When Gibson took over Epiphone fitted most models with "mini humbucking" pickups. A compact version of the Seth Lover-designed Gibson humbucker, these excellent and underrated pickups give a clearer, more trebly response. Mini humbuckers are found on Sheratons, Rivieras, Crestwoods, the Howard Roberts, and others. Gibson later used the same units on the Les Paul Deluxe. Gibson's own single-coil P-90 appeared on several Epiphone models including the solid-body Wilshire, the Les Paul Junior-alike Coronet, and the ES-330-style Casino. There was also a narrow single-coil that powered the Olympic, the Epiphone version of Gibson's budget Melody Maker solid-body.

top > **Epiphone's light, loud Coronet carried a single P-90 pickup.**

above > **Gibson's mini Epiphone humbuckers make great blues pickups.**

gibson's flying v delayed takeoff

"Stodgy"—that was Fender's assessment of Gibson in the late 1950s. Stung into action, Ted McCarty ordered a local firm to help design some guitars that would revolutionize Gibson's image. It came up with three: the Flying V, the Explorer, and the Moderne, and displayed them to its dealers in 1958. The dealers were extremely un-impressed, and the new guitars sold at a crawl. Only 98 Flying Vs left the factory in the 1950s, and less than half that number of Explorers, while none of the semi-mythical third design—the Moderne—have ever been found. Seeing that V's and Explorers are now among the most sought-after vintage guitars of all, the value of an original re-discovered Moderne is unimaginable.

The Flying V's unique combination of edgy power, sweet sustain, unrivaled upper-fret access, and outrageous image has attracted its fair share of blues admirers. Aside from Albert King there's Lonnie Mack, a formative influence on Stevie Ray Vaughan, who played an original 1950s Flying V with an added Bigsby vibrato on his huge 1963 hit "Memphis." Contemporary bluesman Larry McCray uses a sunburst 1967 Flying V re-issue when he needs more cutting edge than his Les Paul Custom can provide.

below > **It's hard to believe that the futuristic Flying V was designed over 40 years ago. This gold-hardware model with its gold logo and black scratchplate was a special 1957 prototype.**

right > **The original patent drawing for the Flying V.**

far right > **Jimi Hendrix's psychedelic-painted 1960s Flying V was re-discovered in England in the 1990s— stripped, but recognizable by the unique fingerprint of the pearl fingerboard inlays.**

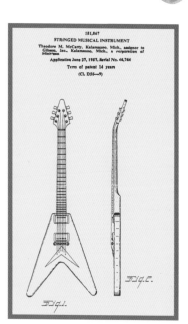

identifier

albert king

The foremost pioneer of the new high-powered blues sound of the 1960s, Albert King was born in Indianola, Mississippi in 1923. King's unmistakable sound came from his instinctive, minimalist sense of timing, his thumbed-downstroke attack, his Acoustic amplifier, and his guitar—a left-handed Flying V, strung right-handed and tuned to a C minor chord in the tradition of Albert Collins and, even earlier, of Skip James. After honing his uniquely savage guitar style in the clubs of St. Louis, King recorded for various Chicago companies but shifted to the legendary Memphis soul label Stax in the late 1960s, cutting classic tracks like "Crosscut Saw," and "Born Under A Bad Sign," and scoring big with the psychedelic rock audience. King named his guitar "Lucy" and even claimed to be B. B. King's cousin; he wasn't, and nor did his playing have B. B.'s delicacy and soul, but this gentle giant was a consummate performer. Albert King died of a heart attack in Memphis in 1992.

flying v history

gibson's original flying v was made of Korina, also known as African limba wood, a lightweight mahoganylike timber. Gibson sold 81 in 1958 and 17 in 1959, and also released some around 1962–1963, made from leftover parts.

in 1966 a re-issue was launched, this time made of mahogany, with a large scratchplate surrounding the pickups. Albert King played a late 1960s version, as did Jimi Hendrix.

in 1971 Gibson launched the "medallion" limited edition Flying V, much like the late-1960s model but with a shorter headstock.

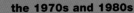

the 1970s and 1980s saw a range of re-designed Vs, including the Flying V II, the Flying V Heritage, and The V. Only in 1990 did Gibson launch a re-issue of the 1950s original, which is still in production.

gibson's current catalog at last includes accurate re-issues of the originals, including the 1959 Korina Flying V and the 1967 Flying V.

above > **1980s variations like The Vee, with its V-shaped pickups and carved laminated body, had little of the charm of the original.**

the gibson firebird **age of speed**

Undaunted by the Flying V's slow sales, Ted McCarty enlisted the aid of Detroit automobile designer Ray Dietrich for Gibson's next foray into the world of guitar fashion—and Dietrich threw the rulebook out of the window. Launched in 1963, the Firebird was Gibson's first-ever guitar with through-neck construction. The central section of three mahogany strips ran from the top to the bottom, flanked at the body end by thinner mahogany wings, saving on weight and giving the guitar a highly unconventional "stepped" look.

The new guitar featured a treble horn that was radically longer than the bass horn and an offset waist—which caused protests from Fender, who claimed copyright on the design. The single-sided headstock was another obvious salute to Fender, but Gibson added its own twist by flipping the headstock over, sculpting the edges, and fitting banjo-style 12:1 ratio Kluson tuners that projected straight outward from the back, thus solving the reverse head's ergonomic shortcomings, and retaining a super-sleek look. A huge, swept-wing scratchplate provided a home for the selector switch, while the pots and jack socket were mounted as on the Gibson SG. though brown and black sunburst was the standard color, a new range of flashy paint finishes including Pelham Blue, Cardinal Red, Kerry Green, Golden Mist, Silver Mist, and Polaris White made the Firebird Gibson's most futuristic looking guitar so far.

the firebird sound

With its ultra-vibrant all-mahogany through-neck construction and specially designed pickups, the new Firebird sounded as great as it looked. Although the Firebird pickup looks much like an Epiphone mini humbucker—though with a solid cover and with no adjustable polepieces—the two designs are very different. The mini humbucker has a single alnico magnet underneath both coils; the Firebird humbucker has two bar magnets running through the center of each coil, with a mild steel plate on the underside.

top > **The ultimate Firebird: a Firebird VII in knock-'em-dead Cardinal Red with a huge swept-wing scratchplate, three gold-plated pickups, and a gold-plated Deluxe vibrato.**

above > **Gibson's super-sharp Firebird humbucker is one of the great underrated blues pickups. This is a replacement unit made by Seymour Duncan.**

Though the Firebird pickup has the same basic EQ as a full-sized humbucker, it has slightly more treble and cleans up well by backing off the volume control, giving a sound somewhere between the Gibson and Fender camps. Other pickup makers—like Seymour Duncan, above—have since latched on to this pickup's unique sound.

identifier

johnny winter

With a manic, propulsive guitar style reminiscent of Elmore James, Gatemouth Brown, and Lightnin' Slim, Mississippi-born Johnny Winter with his Gibson Firebird emerged onto the scene in 1969 and was instantly hailed as the new blues/rock savior. After dallying with hard rock, Winter returned once again to the blues and performed valuable work with Muddy Waters on the master's great comeback LPs of the 1970s, beginning with *Hard Again*. Having honed a high-octane blues trio format and blazed a trail for Stevie Ray Vaughan to follow, Johnny Winter remains a real Texas blues hero.

firebird history

The four original "reverse" Firebirds were introduced in mid 1963 and discontinued in May 1965. Some rare 1965 "transition" models have nonreversed or nonbeveled headstocks with normal right-angled machineheads, while others carry black P-90 pickups:

firebird I: single pickup in the bridge position, one tone and one volume control, no neck binding, dot inlays, compensated one-piece bridge/tailpiece—total sales 1963-1965: 1,377.

firebird III: two pickups and a three-way toggle switch, short flat-armed vibrato, bound fingerboard, dot inlays—total sales: 2,546.

firebird V: two pickups and a three-way toggle, Tune-O-Matic bridge, Deluxe vibrato with tubular arm, engraved tailpiece cover, trapezoid neck inlays—total sales: 925.

firebird VII: three pickups, gold-plated hardware, Deluxe vibrato with Tune-O-Matic bridge, engraved tailpiece cover, block inlays beginning at first fret—total sales: 303.

gibson's nonreverse firebird
backward step

We may never know how much legal pressure Fender exerted, but after just two short years Gibson dropped the original Firebird design. The name survived, however, as the company soon re-launched the range—but with a totally different look. Gone was the "reverse" body shape, to be replaced by a funky if rather amoebalike mahogany slab. Gone was the upside-down headstock with its banjo tuners; gone, too, was the through-neck design with the "stepped" body, with Gibson reverting to its tried-and-tested glued neck construction. Now the fingerboard carried plain dots, and even the electronics were changed, with the original plain-covered pickups now reserved for the top models only; the cheapest two now had soapbar-style single coils.

Launched in 1965, the four "non-reverse" Firebirds were destined to sell poorly. They were too Fenderlike for Gibson players, too

below> **The middle model of the "non-reverse" range, the Firebird III had three black-covered P-90s. Although Gibson had changed the original design after complaints from Fender, the Mk 2 version looked even more like a Fender than before.**

Gibsonlike for Fender players, and too ugly for practically everybody else. A sunburst finish was again standard, but Gibson tried to spice up the pudding by making its full range of 1960s custom colors available. The Firebird I was the base model, with two black-covered P-90 pickups, a stud bridge, and a "short arm" vibrato. The Firebird III was identical save for an extra P-90, bringing the total to three. The twin-pickup Firebird V, the cheapest model with proper mini-humbucking Firebird pickups, gained a Tune-O-Matic bridge and a Deluxe vibrato with an engraved metal tailpiece cover. Top of the range was the new Firebird VII, with the same specifications as the V but with gold-plated parts, and three mini-humbuckers.

Alas, these changes did little to alter the Firebird's faltering sales, and the guitar disappeared in 1969 (only very recently has Gibson revived the design for its Historic Series). Today "nonreverse" Firebirds rate relatively low on the collectability ladder, so for players after a vintage bargain, a higher-end model with the correct pickups will give you the sound—and get you noticed.

clarence "gatemouth" brown

This particular Gibson would have dropped straight off the blues map were it not for Gatemouth Brown and his faithful nonreverse Firebird with its custom-tooled leather pickguard. "Gatemouth was the baddest guitar player I ever saw," says R&B legend Ike Turner, a veteran of many a barroom guitar cutting contest, and a man who should know. "Okie Dokie Stomp... whoo! How does he play that?"

Born in 1924 in Louisiana, but raised in Texas, Brown was—and still is—a killer player, his style an out-of-left-field gumbo of country, blues, jazz, and Texas swing. Weaned on the Count Basie and Duke Ellington big bands, he filled in for T-Bone Walker one night in Houston in 1947 to such great effect that the club owner formed Peacock records just to showcase his talents. Through the 1950s, Brown's extrovert guitar skills were eagerly absorbed by disciples such as Albert Collins and Johnny "Guitar" Watson, and since the 1970s his shows have been fabulously eclectic affairs (Brown is just as likely to play harmonica or saw on his beloved fiddle as to peal off wicked guitar instrumentals). Don't call Gatemouth Brown a blues guitarist—just call him one of the last American originals.

right > **A one-off guitar for a one-off player: Gatemouth Brown and his customized Firebird V.**

gibson's sg slimmed down for the 1960s

The Explorer and the Flying V had proved that Gibson could look to the future. Now they needed a new solidbody guitar to take over from the Les Paul. Though beautiful, the Les Paul was heavy and perhaps even old-fashioned, and the gorgeous flame-topped Standards had been massively outsold by the simple, flat-bodied Les Paul Junior—even more so when, in 1958, Gibson had changed the design to offer not one cutaway, but two.

Gibson's answer to the problem was the SG, a slimmer and far lighter all-mahogany solidbody with devilish-looking twin cutaways and stylish beveled edges. Introduced in 1960, the first SGs still carried the "Les Paul" name (and Les Paul himself was pictured in advertisements for the new guitar). After a couple of years, however, the endorsee's name disappeared; Les Paul claimed that he'd always felt unhappy with the SG's potential structural weakness around the neck join. Tonally, the SG proved to be a more single-minded animal than the Les Paul, though Gibson sought to provide some variation by equipping some models with the Les Paul Standard's humbuckers and others with the Les Paul Junior's single-coil P-90s.

below > **One of the greatest: Earl Hooker in the studio with an SG Standard.**

identifier

sister rosetta tharpe

Sister Rosetta Tharpe may have been an out-and-out gospel performer but she also had a mean, note-bending blues guitar style, rhythmic, staccato, and inventive. Born in Arkansas in 1915, Tharpe moved with her mother to Chicago where she heard not just gospel but also jazz and the blues sounds of Big Bill Broonzy and Memphis Minnie. She first recorded in 1938, and rocked up gospel songs for the Cotton Club and Harlem Apollo audiences using a National Triolian resonator guitar. She picked an early electric guitar on some sessions in 1941, probably an electrified National archtop, then settled on a big, blond Gibson L-5 jazzer to record some of her hardest-rocking tracks. She returned triumphantly to the stage in the 1960s, and there's some wonderful footage of this queen of the gospel shouters burning up the frets on a white Gibson Les Paul/SG. Rosetta Tharpe even toured with Muddy Waters in the early 1970s, and though she suffered much criticism during her life for daring to mix spirituals with blues, she's now recognized as a truly great guitarist—and one of the original soul sisters.

the sg custom

in early 1961 Gibson unveiled the new SG (Solid Guitar), designing the range to accommodate all pockets.

top of the range was the white-painted SG-style Les Paul Custom, with three humbuckers and all the trimmings: a five-piece split diamond headstock inlay, pearl block markers on an ebony fingerboard, and gold-plated hardware including a Tune-O-Matic bridge.

from 1963 the Custom dropped the "Les Paul" name and became the plain SG Custom, while vibrato-fitted models came with the Maestro Vibrola, a unit which worked on a up-and-down principle.

in 1966 the scratchplate was altered to completely surround the pickups, while a walnut finish became standard by 1969.

1970s and 1980s The SG Custom stayed in the range through the 1970s with just a few new finish options, but was dropped in 1980. It was re-issued as the SG Les Paul Custom in 1987 and is still available today

left > **Sister Rosetta Tharpe in full song, playing a handsome white Les Paul/SG Custom through a Vox AC30 amplifier.**

freak power the gibson sg and blues rock

With its super-light weight and with a design that placed the neck well out to the left, giving plenty of access to the upper frets for extended solo workouts, the Gibson SG was ideally placed to make its mark with the blues-influenced rock players of the 1960s.

Frank Zappa—heavily influenced by Johnny "Guitar" Watson—played an SG Special. Carlos Santana ruled San Francisco with another SG Special before he moved on to a Gibson L6S, a Yamaha, and then a Paul Reed Smith. Rolling Stone Mick Taylor alternated between a Gibson 335 and an SG Standard after his original 1958 Les Paul was stolen from London's Whisky A Go Go club. Mostly, however, the SG found its home with the rock fraternity. The revered Timebox/Patto guitarist Ollie Halsall employed a white SG Custom; flamenco-influenced Robbie Krieger from The Doors was a faithful fan, and Pete Townshend of The Who immortalized one at Woodstock in 1969 by smashing it to splinters. He later recalled that he never had any trouble breaking an SG with a single well-aimed swipe as they were "like balsa wood."

above right > **The guitar with the devil's horns: Gibson's light but powerful SG Special proved a perfect tool as blues in the 1960s moved from the cool, sharp 1950s sound toward extended overdriven soloing. This one is in Pelham Blue.**

right > **A 1961 Gibson flyer for the new Les Paul/SG Custom, promising "wonderfully clear bell-like tone that must be heard." Through a Gibson amp with typically low input gain, the SG was indeed clear—but through a hotter amp, the result was a good deal raunchier.**

identifier

clapton's psychedelic sg

One of the most famous SGs of all is the one Eric Clapton played with Cream in the 1960s. Originally a Les Paul/SG—probably a 1961 model, although the serial number has been obliterated—the guitar was specially painted by Simon Posthuma and Marijke Koger, known as The Fool, whose other projects included John Lennon's Rolls-Royce, Jack Bruce's Fender Bass VI, and The Beatles' Apple building in London. Eventually Clapton donated the psychedelic SG to George Harrison, who in turn passed it on to Apple signing Jackie Lomax. A few years later Lomax used the Gibson as surety against a $500 loan from guitarist/producer Todd Rundgren, and Rundgren ended up with the guitar. When last sighted, the SG carried Grover tuners, a 1970s Schaller bridge, and had suffered a number of headstock breaks, but the paintwork remains fully intact—and, perhaps uniquely for such a priceless musical icon, was still in regular use.

standards, specials, and juniors

sg standard, second in line behind the SG Custom, was finished in cherry and carried two full-size humbuckers. Also introduced in early 1961, the Standard carried the "Les Paul" name on the truss-rod cover and featured a Deluxe vibrato with a side-to-side action (not one of Gibson's most valued innovations) until late 1963. Collectors value pre-1965 models most highly: from 1966, the guitar featured a larger scratchplate. The Standard was replaced by the SG Deluxe in 1971.

the twin p-90 sg special was next in the 1961 line, available in a cherry or white finish. After the same vibrato and scratchplate alterations as the Standard, the Special was replaced by the SG Pro in 1971, then re-issued again in the 1970s with various hardware changes.

the les paul junior, the most affordable of all, was a minimal but stylish budget model in a cherry finish with a single P-90. The guitar was re-named the SG Jr in Gibson's catalog from late 1963. There was also an SG TV version with a white finish that lasted until 1968, just three years before the eventual demise of the SG Jr.

right > **The resonant little SG Jr gives fine vintage rock/blues sounds on a budget.**

gibson's double-neck
monster blues

Gibson's behemoth, the double-neck guitar—a progressive rock icon, sure, but a blues instrument? Gibson was not first on the double-neck scene, but the EDS-1275 of 1958 compensated for its tardiness with sheer quality. The body shape and construction were unique for the company, with small, sharp pointed cutaways, a hollowed-out maple body to save as much weight as possible, and a carved spruce top for the best possible response. Various neck combinations were available, including bass, mandolin, short-scale six-string guitar, and four-string tenor guitar, the most popular carrying a six-string neck with a 12-string neck above it. The remarkable Earl Hooker, a man with the habit of turning up with the latest, flashiest guitars in the whole of Chicago, played a later-type EDS-1275 with a solid mahogany SG-shaped body.

left > **Gibson's massive
EDS-1275 double-neck,
1958. These early custom-
order models with the
carved spruce tops are the
best double-necks Gibson
made.**

"I'd been trying to play slide, but then I heard Earl Hooker playing behind Muddy Waters…and I gave him my slide! He was an all-rounder, the best I ever saw. He could play like Muddy, like Elmore, like Robert Nighthawk. One time he made me cry. He really did."

buddy guy

identifier

earl hooker

A native of Clarksdale, Mississippi, Earl Zebedee Hooker was a lifetime wanderer who possessed one of the most beautiful slide guitar styles of all time. A cousin of John Lee Hooker, but influenced primarily by the legendary slide specialist Robert Nighthawk, Hooker paid his dues alongside Sonny Boy Williamson and Ike Turner, and first recorded at Memphis' Sun Studios around the same time as Elvis. In the early 1960s he became part of producer Mel London's studio band, cutting many fabulous guitar showcases including his best-known instrumental, "Blue Guitar" (confusingly, this track was used to back Muddy Waters on "You Shook Me," a song later covered by Led Zeppelin—who based "Whole Lotta Love" on another Hooker co-composition, "You Need Love"). Hooker played in standard tuning, not open, and experimented freely with his sound; he played Danelectro double-necks as well as Gibsons, and even used the dreaded wah-wah to great effect. The king of the slide guitar sidemen died of TB in 1970 aged 41.

below > **Arhoolie records captured the double-neck-toting slide master on fine form in the late 1960s on** *The Moon Is Rising* **and** *Two Bugs And A Roach*.

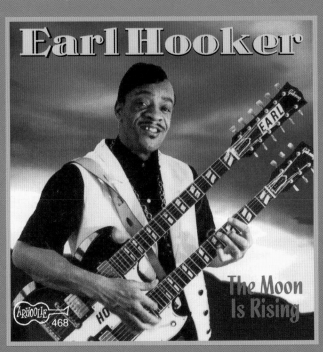

double trouble

6/12 string The Gibson EDS-1275 6/12 string first became available in 1958 on a custom-order basis. It carried four humbuckers, two control knobs for each neck, and three selector switches—two for pickup selection and a third for neck selection.

other neck combinations EDS-1275s from the first four years of production, combining a hollow maple body and hand-carved solid spruce top, are the most desirable. There was also a "double mandolin" version, the EMS-1235, with a standard six-string neck and a short "octave guitar" neck, and a later guitar/bass model, the EBSF-1250. Most combination of necks was available, including two six-string necks for different tunings or even mandolin or tenor guitar necks.

simpler construction In 1962 Gibson dropped the EDS-1275's expensive combination of maple and spruce, and changed to a simpler solid mahogany construction much like that of an SG guitar, complete with beveled edges. Though discontinued in 1968, the EDS-1275 was re-introduced in the late 1970s following exposure in various progressive rock bands and particularly in the hands of Jimmy Page (below).

harmony sovereign *poor man's gibson*

Harmony's Sovereign guitar was widely used by many "re-discovered" blues stars and many new players in the fast-rising 1960s folk-blues scene. With spruce tops, mahogany backs and sides and a unique body style somewhere between a Martin dreadnought and a Gibson jumbo, Sovereigns were loud, quirkily handsome, and reassuringly cheap. The top of the line model cost around $70, while lesser Harmony acoustics could be had for $40. Until the Asian invasion of the 1970s, the Sovereign was one of the bestselling guitars in the US. Harmony also sold a vast range of smaller, even more affordable flat-top and archtop guitars. These Colorama and Caribbean models tend to be more decorative than strictly practical, but some retro-fixated guitarists still use them today—like Bob Log, the hollering, space-helmet wearing one-man blues band.

Harmony, meanwhile, owned the Stella name, seemingly knowing or caring little of the guitars' legendary blues status nor of Leadbelly and his Stella 12-string. It did manufacture a hefty 12-string Stella-badged guitar much like the Sovereign—indeed, Blind Willie McTell played one of these on his last-ever recordings—but with unerring bad timing Harmony dropped all 12-string production in 1958, missing out on the rocketing folk guitar market.

right > **Robert Pete Williams with a DeArmond-equipped Sovereign.**

above right > **Harmony's 1960s flat-tops fit right into the "whatever's cheap and available" blues tradition. This range-topping sunburst Deluxe Sovereign offered a fancy pin bridge and double pickguards.**

right > **These unique, visionary prison recordings from 1959 were an influence on Ry Cooder and Captain Beefheart.**

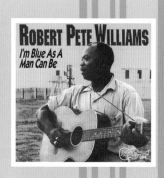

harmony men

Two of the greatest blues discoveries of the 1960s both played Harmony Sovereigns. Mance Lipscomb, born just before the turn of the century in Texas, became one of the best-loved performers on the blues festival scene after making his first recordings in 1960 at the grand old age of 65. Not strictly a bluesman, more a songster, Lipscomb delivered everything—blues, spirituals, pop songs, ballads, and stories—in a warm, genial style.

Robert Pete Williams was another unclassifiable acoustic blues stylist. Born in 1914, he played around Baton Rouge, Louisiana but in 1956 he ended up in Angola State Penitentiary after killing a man in a barroom brawl. Two ethnomusicologists, Dr Harry Oster and Richard Allen, impressed both by Williams' unique free-form guitar style and his plea of self-defense, negotiated his release after just three years. Though initially limited to playing within the Louisiana state border, Williams' deep, powerful storytelling made a huge impression. Freed to travel, Williams teamed up with Mississippi Fred McDowell and remained a popular live draw until his death in 1980.

identifier

the last harmonys

Along with numerous cheap Stellas—distinguished from Oscar Schmidt models by the lack of underlining under the headstock logo—Harmony made an ever-expanding range of acoustic flat-tops, many of them with solid tops.

early 1960s Top Harmony acoustics were the Sovereign 1260 and the smaller model 1203, both costing $72, with solid spruce tops, pinless bridges, and slim re-inforced necks. Several 000-sized Grand Concert versions like the 162 and all-mahogany 165 both cost about $40. After a few years Harmony offered a new sunburst-finished deluxe Sovereign, the 1265, with an imitation tortoiseshell headstock facing and a double pickguard.

early 1970s Acoustic lineup expanded to almost 20 variations, including the black-finished H1264, the sunburst H1266, and the natural H1260. The Grand Concert H1203 and H1204 were very decent players' guitars, the H1204 was a popular all-black model with ornate pickguard, while the H159 was an affordable, $50 Stella-badged Sovereign-shaped jumbo. The priciest guitar, at $170, was the luxury H1266 Sovereign Deluxe Jumbo.

right > **Harmony-made Stella 12-string, late 1940s. Blind Willie McTell played an identical guitar on his last-ever recordings.**

gretsch guitars **rare blues birds**

It's a mystery why Gretsch guitars have been so seldom used for blues. Take a great guitar like the Duo Jet: Like a Les Paul but semi-solid, and used so brilliantly by Gene Vincent's guitarist Cliff Gallup and, later, George Harrison; or the semi-acoustic 6120, one of the ultimate country and rock'n'roll guitars, as displayed by Eddie Cochran and Brian Setzer. There was nothing wrong with Gretsch's pickups; the single-coil DeArmonds of the 1950s, the post-'58 humbucking Filter'Trons and the single-coil HiLo'Trons of the 1960s all sounded fine, in very different ways. Maybe the explanation lies with Gretsch's close association with the country market and with Nashville guitar star Chet Atkins.

Yet a few rare blues guitarists have played Gretsches. J. B. Lenoir, a fine boogie rhythm player who sang politically charged originals like "Tax Paying Blues," "Korea Blues," and "Alabama March" in a distinctive high-pitched voice, played an archtop Gretsch Synchromatic with "cats eye" soundholes and an added pickup. And of course there's Mississippi-born Bo Diddley, living link between Delta blues and Chuck Berry and the originator of perhaps the greatest rock'n'roll beat of all time, whose outrageous, fuzzed-up guitar work on his custom-made rectangular Gretsches laid the groundwork for everyone from Jimi Hendrix to the Rolling Stones.

above right > **Blues players of the 1940s and 1950s often got hold of Gretsch archtop acoustics. This is an early Gretsch Synchromatic archtop with cats eye soundholes and a "stairstep" bridge.**

right > **Bo Diddley, rock trailblazer and patent-holder of the "shave and a haircut—two bits" rhythm, with one of his many custom Gretsches.**

lowell fulson

One of the great blues all-rounders, Lowell Fulson—born in 1921 in Tulsa, Oklahoma—usually played a red tailpiece-equipped Gibson 335, but back in the 1960s he was often pictured with the emperor of all Gretsch guitars, the glamorous, gold-plated White Falcon. Fulson recorded his first hits in the 1940s on the West Coast (1948's "Three O'Clock Blues" was adopted by B. B. King, as was "Every Day I Have The Blues"). A brief affair with Aladdin was followed by a longer relationship with Chess, where he laid down numbers like "Check Yourself," "Do Me Right," "Trouble, Trouble," and his trademark tune "Reconsider Baby," later covered by Elvis. Fulson might have missed the boat to real fame, but over five full decades he has turned his hand to many great styles from country blues to funky soul, and his knife-sharp solos—dug out with a thumbpick—are always great value.

identifier

dating gretsch

Dating Gretsch guitars can be a complicated business. The serial number system is fallible, and Gretsch made many minor design and hardware changes to their instruments, sometimes on an almost monthly basis. There's a new number system in place on the current Japanese-made Gretsch series.

1950–1965
numbers on label inside guitar

1950 3000s
1951 4000-5000
1952 5000-6000
1953 6000-8000
1954 9000-12000
1955 12000-16000
1956 17000-21000
1957 22000-26000
1958 27000-30000
1959 30000-34000
1960 34000-39000
1961 39000-45000
1962 46000-52000
1963 53000-63000
1964 63000-77000
1965 77000-84000

1965–1972
Numbers on back of headstock: the first one or two digits indicate the month of manufacture, the next digit indicates the last digit of the year, and the remaining digits show the number of instruments made up to that point in that year. The legend 'Made in USA' next to a number means a guitar made between 1967 and 1973.

1973–1981
Numbering system is as above, but a hyphen separates the 'month' from the 'year' digits.

gibson's babies mahogany blues

More and more players have come to appreciate Gibson's small bodied acoustics of the 1960s; character-crammed spruce/mahogany construction gave a warm, lively tone—some models were straight-braced, not X-braced—while Gibson's short 24 ¾ in. scale length made for an ideal fingerpicking blues guitar. True, these guitars are not as fine as the lightly-built Nick Lucas and L-00 models of the 1930s, but those guitars have long been elevated to near-mythical status, with prices to match. Even the most affordable prewar Gibson-made flat-tops—like Kalamazoos, much like the Gibson-badged equivalents but lacking a truss rod—have changed from being considered semi-disposable to reasonably sought-after. No-one's going to pretend that Gibson's compact postwar acoustics possess anything like the mighty, crisp response of a long-scale rosewood-bodied Martin dreadnought on full song, but LG-1s, LG-2s, and even 1960s B-25s and LG-0s were the choice of many blues guitarists including Johnny Shines, Pink Anderson, and Furry Lewis. Today they offer plenty of vibe for the buck and a taste of that all-important blues heritage.

above > **With a short scale and a warm but funky sound, small-bodied Gibsons like this early 1960s LG-1 can make decent blues fingerpickers.**

left > **This delicately shaped Gibson L-C Century of 1934 shows how much Gibson's small body design had changed in 30 years. The guitar was part of a special pearloid-fingerboard range commemorating the "Century Of Progress" exhibition at Chicago's World Fair.**

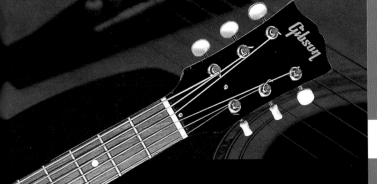

johnny shines

Though like many of his contemporaries, Johnny Shines' career seemed to be played out in the shadow of Robert Johnson, Shines knew Johnson well, having traveled and played with him for from 1935 to 1937. Born in Frayser, Tennessee in 1915, Shines grew up listening to Lonnie Johnson and Blind Lemon Jefferson. He picked up the guitar in 1932 after meeting his greatest inspiration, Howlin' Wolf, and was making his living as a musician within a year. After recording some fine tracks in Chicago after the war, Shines went back to construction work—he pawned all his guitars and amps for $100—but returned in 1966 for a British recording session (he claimed he hadn't played for seven years). Over the next 25 years, Johnny Shines and his guitar—a National on 1971's Traditional Delta Blues, otherwise a humble 1960s Gibson B-25—extended the Johnson legacy with power, integrity, and soul.

identifier

the lg series

Driven by a need to save timber, Gibson launched its long-running LG small acoustic series in 1942 with the 14 ⅛ wide, sunburst finished, X-braced mahogany/spruce LG-2. The LG-2 had a sweet, balanced sound and dropped Gibson's V-shaped prewar neck profile in favor of a new, more rounded shape. Due to wartime restrictions some examples had no truss-rods, while others successfully employed mahogany tops.

1946–1947 The LG-1 of 1947 was a slightly cheaper, straight-braced version, while the top LG-3 model, introduced in 1946, retained the LG-2's X-bracing but offered multiple binding and a natural-finish top.

1958 The inexpensive LG-0, introduced in 1958, was an extra-affordable mahogany-topped version with ladder bracing. Bright sounding if a little light in the bass, these guitars went out of production in 1974.

In **1963** the LG-3 became the B-25N—Johnny Shines' guitar—still with a natural top but a slightly narrower neck, while the sunburst LG-2 became the sunburst B-25 (some late LG-3s and early B-25s have plastic bridges, and are best avoided). The LG-1 survived the name-changing and remained popular until the early 1970s. Both B-25s and their 12-string sibling were also discontinued in the mid 1970s.

gibson's j-45 and j-50
folk blues classics

Gibson's "round-shouldered" flat-tops—the Southerner Jumbo, its 1960s equivalent the Country Western, the sunburst J-45, and its natural-top sister the J-50—were real stalwarts of the 1960s folk scene and used by dozens of revered blues artists from Lightnin' Hopkins to Mississippi John Hurt, and the Reverend Robert Wilkins. In fact, practically every acoustic blues player seems to have used a Gibson flat-top at some point in the 1950s and 1960s.

Severe timber shortages during World War Two, meant many early models came with maple backs and sides instead of mahogany. As the years rolled by, however, the J-45 and J-50 underwent only minor tweaks: a change of decal here, a black center-seam there, the odd aesthetic adjustment to the bridge design, and some alterations to the bracing around 1955. Today, these sweet, warm-toned, honest-sounding guitars are as popular as ever. Bluesman John Campbell, for instance, employs a 1952 Gibson SJ with a DeArmond pickup, while lap-style slide player Kelly Joe Phelps uses a 1945 J-45.

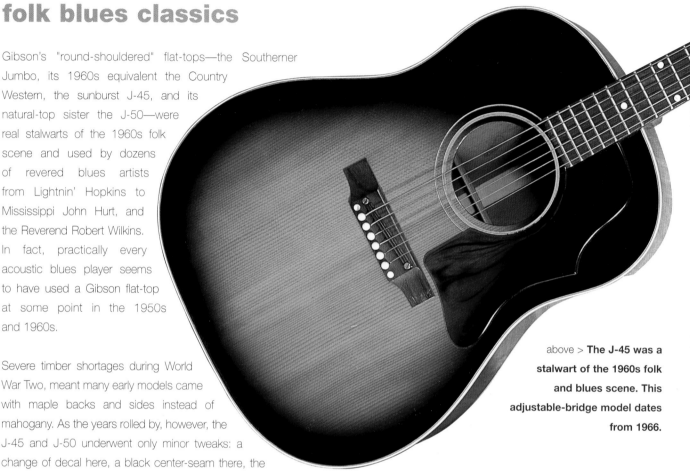

above > **The J-45 was a stalwart of the 1960s folk and blues scene. This adjustable-bridge model dates from 1966.**

right > **Eric Bibb is one of the new breed of blues players to re-discover the characterful Gibson acoustic sound.**

j-50 blues

One guitar, two very different styles. Lightnin' Hopkins, born in 1912 in Centerville, Texas, was lucky enough to meet and play with Blind Lemon Jefferson. He played for nickels on the streets of Houston before landing a deal with the LA-based Aladdin label in the late 1940s and scoring big hits with "Shotgun Blues," "Abilene," and "Big Mama Jump." By the mid1950s Hopkins' star was waning, but in 1959 he dropped his electric guitar for acoustic and before long his deeply emotional, free-form style caught on big with the coffee-house crowd of the 1960s.

John Jackson, another Gibson acoustic devotee, perfected his ragtime-tinged Piedmont blues around his home of Woodville, Virginia during the 1940s. Emerging into the public eye during the folk revival after nearly 20 years of silence, Jackson chose a natural-top J-50 for its warm bass and slim neck, and soon made a name as a warm, convivial songster with a wonderful ability to invoke the fingerpicking styles of his heroes, Willie Walker, Blind Blake, and Blind Boy Fuller.

below > **Mississippi fingerpicker John Jackson with his Gibson.**

identifier

j-45 and j-50 timeline

1942 J-45 introduced with 16 in. wide mahogany body, dark sunburst spruce top, 24 ¾ in. scale, mahogany neck with pearl-dotted rosewood fingerboard, belly-down bridge with two pearl dots, "firestripe" pickguard.

1943–44 Some with "wartime" woods: maple back and sides, some with mahogany tops or no truss-rods and rectangular bridge.

1946 Bridge changes from rectangular to belly-shaped; natural-top J-50 introduced.

1949 Bridge reverses so that "belly" points upward.

1950 Triple-bound top.

1955 Tall scalloped bracing changes to short, non-scalloped type; pickguard altered from teardrop-shape to single-point design.

1956 Adjustable bridge (J-45ADJ and J-50ADJ) optional.

1962 No pearl dots on bridge, and the J-45 receives a new-look cherry sunburst.

1968 Some with black or cherry tops, some with screwed-down "Gibson" logo pickguards.

1969 Round-shoulder body shape changes to square-shouldered. The J-45 and J-50 were discontinued in 1982, but the J-45 was brought back in 1984, and has remained in production ever since, with new vintage re-issue and rosewood-bodied versions.

above > **Martin killer: the super-loud long-scale rosewood-bodied Advanced Jumbo was one of the finest Gibson flat-tops of all time.**

the gibson j-200 blond ambition

The J-200 represents the very pinnacle of Gibson's jumbo-sized guitars. A huge 17 in. wide and decorated with fancy inlays, an open "moustache" style bridge, and an ornate engraved pickguard, this all-conquering flat-top was introduced as the SJ-200 in 1938, and the 96 prewar examples all came with rosewood backs and sides instead of the later maple. In fact the guitar had been designed for country star Ray Whitley, and it soon became a must-have accessory for all Hollywood cowboys and Grand Ole Opry superstars through the 1940s and 1950s. A J-200 cost exactly $200—and for an extra $50 you could have your name inlaid, country-style, down the fingerboard.

Though the J-200 excelled as a rhythm guitar, its outstanding volume, rich bass, and the famously balanced Gibson response also made it a hit with some of the most accomplished finger-pickers in the blues world. The Reverend Gary Davis played one, as did the excellent Blind Blake-style Delta fingerpicker Richard "Hacksaw" Harney. Mance Lipscomb was an occasional J-200 user, while the wonderful Skip James used a Gibson J-185—a slightly smaller-bodied version—in the 1960s.

above > **The undisputed king of the flat-tops, Gibson's huge J-200 excels at rhythm and also—in the right hands—at flat picking and fingerpicking blues. This fine blond J-200N was built in 1952.**

right > **King of the fingerpickers: Reverend Gary Davis recording in the 1960s with one of his succession of brand-new Gibson J-200s.**

left > **This 1960s/1970s compilation shows the Texas songster playing a sunburst Gibson J-200 with an added soundhole pickup.**

reverend gary davis

Was the Reverend Gary Davis the finest ragtime/blues guitarist of his generation? Some would say yes—and that includes his one-time students Ry Cooder and Stefan Grossman. Born partially blind in 1896, Davis lived and played in South Carolina between the wars, building up a huge repertoire of blues, spirituals, jazz, and comedy songs by his early 1920s. Ordained as a minister in 1937, he moved to New York in the early 1940s and began a long, successful career as a Harlem street-singer, seamlessly mixing gospel material with secular numbers. Several appearances at the Newport Folk Festival cemented his popularity in the blues revival field, and his still-potent fingerpicking skills made his Bronx home a magnet for many eager young players bearing tape-recorders. Davis' best-known guitar was the blond Gibson J-200 he bore through the 1960s, though he also employed a 12-string Gibson B-45-12.

identifier

j-200 timeline

1938 The SJ-200 is introduced with a 16 ⅞ in. wide and 4 ½ in. deep body, rosewood back and sides, sunburst-finished spruce top with "double X" bracing, ebony "moustache" bridge, scratchplate with engraved flowers, maple neck with ebony fingerboard, and pearl "cloud" fingerboard markers.

1941 Fingerboard changes to rosewood.

1947 Re-named J-200 and supplied with maple back and sides.

1948 Available in natural finish as J-200N.

1961 Bridge changes to include electric-style Tune-O-Matic insert. Body increases in depth, sometimes to as much as 5 in., a new and tonally suspect suspended brace is added under the top: most have now been removed.

1963 Three-piece neck changes to narrower five-piece type.

1969 Height-adjustable bridge as standard.

1971 Gibson switch back to ebony fingerboard (back to rosewood in 1979) and revert to heavy "double x" bracing. Bridge changes to solid style with no cut-outs.

1984 The J-200 returns to original 1950's specifications, and has continued to be made ever since.

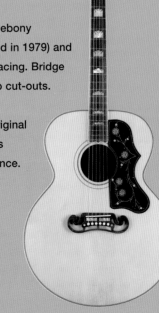

right > **A current Montana-made Gibson SJ-200 re-issue.**

national res-o-glas guitars
plastic fantastics

Valco's National and Supro-badged electrics were some of the wildest and strangest guitars of their time, and both the futuristic fiberglass versions and the slightly more traditional wooden-bodied models found users in the blues world. The company's literature of the time was a masterpiece of extended hyperbole. "The graceful construction is of the new space age wonder material—Res-O-Glas," it promised. "The gleaming velvet-smooth finish is climatically immune, and won't stain or check…The precision Vista-Power pickups are separately adjustable for elevation, and the exclusive Val-Trol system of separate tone and volume controls for each switch position is easily preset." This last feature was indeed unique, allowing the player separate control over the middle "both pickups on" switch position. Alas, these guitars were neither easy to produce nor as profitable as expected, and they lasted only a few years. Today, these unorthodox devices have attained a collectable status unimaginable a few years ago, with the most desirable models fetching a couple of thousand dollars.

above> **A glorious half-dozen fiberglass-body Nationals. Back row, left to right: a white Val-Pro 84 with a Silver-Sound bridge, a resonator-equipped Folk Star, a red Val-Pro 82, a black Val-Pro 88, and a white Glenwood 99. Front: a National Studio 66.**

left > **This top-of-the-line National Glenwood 98 has "Silver-Sound"—a contact pickup located in the bridge for an acoustic-style tone.**

identifier

the white stripes

Call it what you like—punk/blues, Zep-a-billy—but the fact is that guitarist Jim White of guitar/drums combo The White Stripes loves Robert Johnson, Son House, Muddy Waters, and Howlin' Wolf, and often plays covers of Blind Willie McTell songs. Jim White's number one guitar is a fabulously bluesy red Res-O-Glas electric, an Airline-labeled variation originally sold by Montgomery Ward, together with an authentic 100-watt Sears Silvertone amp that, he claims, sounds like cardboard.

below > **The White Stripes' Jim White, re-defining electric blues for the post-grunge generation on his Airline guitar.**

silver sound

national, supro, and airline Fiberglass-bodied Valco-made National, Supro, and Airline guitars were introduced in 1962, and could cost more than a Fender Stratocaster—one of the reasons they were discontinued in 1965. Valco also made amplifiers under the same trade names, some with up-to-the-minute features. Some Supro amps had reverb and tremolo by 1956, a full eight years before Fender.

color and finish The Res-O-Glas models were available in four colors—red, black, white, and seafoam green. The wooden-bodied Westwood 75 came in a sunburst finish. The Pro-True necks were re-inforced with magnesium and came with a "zero fret," intended to improve action and intonation.

the nine "map-shaped" guitars included the red, single-pickup Val-Pro 82 with a preset-selecting tone switch, the white 84 model with "Silver-Sound"—an added pickup hidden in the bridge—and the black 88 model with an extra master volume, giving a row of seven knobs all in a straight line. The red Glenwood 95, the white Glenwood 98, and the green Glenwood 99 were the flagship models, distinguished by fancy neck markers, two rows of three knobs with an added master volume, a pointed lower cutaway, and an extra "bite" taken out of the body near the jack socket.

supro guitars are easily distinguished from their National-badged brethren: the "lumps" on National headstocks pointed toward the floor, while Supro headstocks pointed toward the ceiling.

martin in the 1960s
country blues revival

The sound of the Martin dreadnought—a clean, powerful treble and a strong bottom end, ideal for flat-picked rhythm and counterpoint bass lines—formed the backbone of the country music sound from the Carter family through to Hank Williams. Even Elvis thrashed a Martin. Through the 1950s, Martin guitars rose again as the darlings of the new folk revival: Norman Blake, The Kingston Trio, and many more all chose to play instruments built in Nazareth, Pennsylvania, including the guitars that have always formed the backbone of Martin's dreadnought line, the mahogany-bodied D-18, and the rosewood-bodied D-28.

Before long, the guitars so highly prized in the folk arena began to trickle back into blues recordings—some of them loaned to players who had not performed in earnest for many years (Stefan Grossman, the country blues revivalist, lent his own vintage Martins to a number of returning blues artists). Some players, it's true, had always been Martin followers: Josh White, for instance, toured the new 1960s college circuit with his beloved 12-fret 00-21 and a 00-45, often fitted with an extra scratchplate to protect the top.

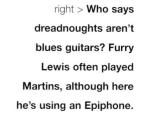

right > **Who says dreadnoughts aren't blues guitars? Furry Lewis often played Martins, although here he's using an Epiphone.**

above > **Martin's rosewood-bodied D-28 is one of the all-time great guitar designs.**

right > **Modern Martins have regained much of the quality of old. This is a herringbone-bound Vintage Series HD-28V.**

identifier

furry lewis

From the 1920s to the 1960s, Walter "Furry" Lewis rose early in the morning to collect garbage cans on the streets of Memphis. Lewis, born sometime before the turn of the century, had once been a valued local blues player. W. C. Handy, the "father of the blues," had given him a Martin guitar, and Lewis used it to record classics like 1928's "Kassie Jones," a six-minute epic that occupied both sides of a 78 r.p.m. record. Although Lewis gave up music in the 1930s when the market for country blues collapsed, he was coaxed back into playing by folklorist Sam Charters in the late 1950s and soon he was delighting audiences once more with his warm storytelling and his dazzlingly expressive fingerpicking and bottleneck guitar styles. Before he passed away in 1981, Lewis introduced a new generation to a cache of songs that had got within an inch of being lost forever.

serial numbers

This list shows the serial number of the last Martin guitar built in every year from 1900 to 2002. The D-28 changed from Brazilian to Indian rosewood around number 250000:

Year	Serial	Year	Serial	Year	Serial
1900	8348	1935	61947	1970	271633
1901	8716	1936	65176	1971	294270
1902	9528	1937	68865	1972	313302
1903	9810	1938	71866	1973	333873
1904	9988	1939	74061	1974	353387
1905	10120	1940	76734	1975	371828
1906	10329	1941	80013	1976	388800
1907	10727	1942	83107	1977	399625
1908	19883	1943	86724	1978	440780
1909	11018	1944	90149	1979	419900
1910	11203	1945	93623	1980	430300
1911	11413	1946	98158	1981	436474
1912	11565	1947	103468	1982	439627
1913	11281	1948	108269	1983	446101
1914	12047	1949	112961	1984	453300
1915	12209	1950	117961	1985	460575
1916	12390	1951	122799	1986	468175
1917	12988	1952	128436	1987	476216
1918	13450	1953	134501	1988	483952
1919	14512	1954	141345	1989	493279
1920	15848	1955	147328	1990	503309
1921	16758	1956	153225	1991	512487
1922	17839	1957	159061	1992	522655
1923	19891	1958	165576	1993	535223
1924	22008	1959	171047	1994	551696
1925	24116	1960	175689	1995	570434
1926	28689	1961	181297	1996	592930
1927	34435	1962	187384	1997	624799
1928	37568	1963	193327	1998	668796
1929	40843	1964	199626	1999	724077
1930	45317	1965	207030	2000	780500
1931	49589	1966	217215	2001	845644
1932	52590	1967	230095	2002	916759
1933	55084	1968	241925		
1934	58679	1969	256003		

martin's 000 and om
fingerstyle classics

While there's no reason why dreadnoughts cannot be excellent blues guitars, few doubt that Martin's smaller models—the 00, the 000, and the 000's long-scale sister, the "OM" Orchestra Model—provide a better balance and response for country-style blues finger-picking. Even all-mahogany 1940s and 1950s models such as the 00-17, which were virtually unsaleable in the 1970s, are now appreciated for their sweet tone and excellent recording characteristics.

Martins have often been used by top blues artists. Muddy Waters used a mahogany 000-18 to record his back-to-the-roots *Folksinger* album (a young Buddy Guy on backup guitar played a Kay archtop). Old-time picker Sylvester Weaver, originator of the famous "Steel Guitar Rag," is reputed to have employed a Martin 000-28. Lonnie Johnson, of course, played an 00-21, while veteran Memphis entertainer Frank Stokes chose another medium-sized model, an 00-28. These days, little remains of Martin's strong one-time association with country music. When not pummeling a vintage National John Hammond plays a mahogany Martin M-18, while award-winning blues artist Rory Block depends upon her vintage re-issue Martin OM-28.

above > **Perhaps the most perfectly balanced-sounding flat-top design of all, Martin's long-scale Orchestra Model had 14 frets to the body and was introduced in 1929. This rare example was made in 1930.**

right > **Josh White with his Martin 00-21.**

identifier

brownie mcghee

Harmonica player Sonny Terry and guitarist Walter "Brownie" McGhee may not have been the best of friends in real life—by the 1970s, they were reluctant even to share a stage—but their 40-year musical partnership helped keep the Piedmont blues tradition alive. McGhee, born in 1915 in Knoxville, Tennessee, was a student of guitarist Blind Boy Fuller, and even toured as "Blind Boy Fuller No. 2" soon after Fuller's death in 1941. Though he recorded for many labels in the 1950s, including some very modern full-electric band numbers, McGhee is best remembered for the way he blended his able acoustic guitar picking with Terry's signature whooping harp sound on old-time classics like "John Henry," and "Pick A Bale Of Cotton." The two were among the first blues visitors to Europe, and their engaging style soon became familiar on the festival circuit. Sonny Terry passed away in 1982 and McGhee followed some 14 years later. It was the end of a genuine blues institution.

blues martins

Martin has responded to a growing appreciation for its classic smaller-bodied models, and as well as making fine replicas of the OM design they've introduced a number of limited-edition blues-oriented signature models. The Eric Clapton-endorsed 000-28EC and 000-42EC guitars both met with widespread acclaim, while Jonny Lang's JLJCR, Keb' Mo's herringbone HD-28, and Kenny Wayne Shephard's JC-16 all carry the blues signature trend into the twenty-first century. Meanwhile, there's a growing market in carefully hand-crafted Martin OM-style guitars from makers such as Schoenberg, Collins, Santa Cruz, Bourgeois, and Merrill.

For shallower pockets, Martin also makes modern equivalents of its Depression-era classics. Basic models such as the slot-head 12-fret 00-15 are very lightly built with mahogany backs, sides, and tops, giving a dry, snappy sound with plenty of bite and character.

right > **Martin's 000-sized guitars are much the same as the OM, but have a shorter and more blues-friendly scale length. This is the Clapton-endorsed 000-28ECB.**

left > **Martin magic: bluesman Brownie McGhee with folk singer Joan Baez.**

guild guitars from the ashes of epiphone

Epiphone fans had a new name to follow from 1952. When the company moved production from New York to Philadelphia following a damaging period of union dissent, a number of key workers chose to throw in their new lot with a brand-new New York concern founded by one-time accordion importer Alfred Dronge and ex-Epiphone sales manager George Mann. Dronge and Mann styled Guild guitars along traditional lines, concentrating first upon refining the familiar electrified archtop template. In fact a number of distinctive features were carried over from Epiphone, including a five-piece neck construction, the distinctive triangle-inside-a-rectangle pearl fingerboard markers, and, on the three-pickup electric models, a row of six rather awkward push-button pickup selectors.

Though the Guild name carried less cachet than that of Gibson, the company's high-quality guitars with its trademark "G shield" headstock inlays and harp-shaped tailpieces soon gained a good reputation—and are highly underrated blues guitars today. A successful series of acoustic flat-tops was also introduced in the early 1960s, with models ranging from big, beefy-sounding dreadnoughts to large and small jumbos, and smaller-bodied guitars such as the all-mahogany M-20, as used by English finger-picker Nick Drake.

above > **Guild's under-appreciated archtops from the 1950s make fine jazz and blues guitars. This top of the line X-550 Stuart was built in 1958.**

left > **The natural-finish X-550 was re-named the X-500B in 1960, gained humbuckers in 1963, and a master volume control in 1971. This one dates from 1974.**

space age muddy waters

By and large Guild's guitar designs followed Gibson and Epiphone's lead, but its first-ever solid-body guitars, the Thunderbird S-200, Polara S-100, and Jet-Star S-50, were futuristic rockers with a unique selling point, a fold-out arm that enabled the guitar to stand upright by itself (most of the time), plus slider switches for extra tonal variation. When the Muddy Waters band signed a short-lived endorsement deal with Guild in the mid 1960s, their leader adopted these strange beasts. Waters actually owned two Guild Thunderbird S-200s—both single-coil models, one red, one brown—and used them on a number of tours. It must be one of the most unusual guitars to be used by a real blues master.

identifier

guild's first archtops

X-175 The cheapest in the line came with two soapbar pickups. All Guild archtops changed to humbuckers in the 1960s, while scale lengths altered from 25.5 in. to 24.75 in.

X-350 Essentially a smaller version of the Epiphone Emperor, the Stratford 350 (X indicates an electric model) carried three white-cover single-coil pickups and the clunky push-button selector system. The X-350 came in sunburst: the X-375 was the natural-finish equivalent.

X500 The X-500 was a more upmarket model. It employed the same elegant 17 in. wide body as the 350 but came with multiple body binding, bound f-holes, Epiphone-style fingerboard markers and just two pickups linked to a Gibson-style three-way toggle switch. The X-550 was the natural-finished version and was often made of the finest curly maple.

serial numbers Guild serial numbers can be complex, but this partial list shows the numbers of the last guitar manufactured in each year of Guild's first three decades:

1952 350		**1962** 22722		**1972** 75602
1953 840		**1963** 28943		**1973** 95496
1954 1526		**1964** 38636		**1974** 112803
1955 2468		**1965** 4660		**1975** 130304
1956 3830		**1966** 46608		**1976** 149625
1957 5712		**1967** 46637		**1977** 169867
1958 8348		**1968** 46656		**1978** 195067
1959 12035		**1969** 46696		**1979** 211877
1960 14713		**1970** 50978		
1961 18419		**1971** 61463		

left > **Out of place: Muddy Waters thumbpicking one of his Guild Thunderbird electrics.**

guild's semi-acoustics
working-class heroes

Guild reached out to the rock'n'roll and blues worlds in the late 1950s with the T-100 and twin-pickup T-100D guitars, plus a great-sounding if little-recognized range of amplifiers. The early T-100D or "Slim Jim" was a thinline hollow-body semi-acoustic with two fat-sounding "Frequency Tested" single-coil pickups much like Gibson P-90s; light and comfortable, these new guitars were capable of raucous sounds when put through the right amplifier.

Meanwhile, 1960 saw the launch of the similar but long-scaled Starfire semi, which in 1963 gained Guild's own excellent-sounding-sounding humbuckers and a sister model, a 335-type double cutaway design. Another great Guild was the semi-hollow M-75 Aristocrat, a small-bodied single-cutaway guitar combining easy handling with rich response thanks to a semi-solid construction with a solid spruce top. The M-75 came with a 23 ¼ in. scale ("the new popular short-action professional scale," boasted Guild), gold hardware, and block inlays. Though dropped from the catalog in 1962 it re-appeared in 1967, re-named the Bluesbird—making it perhaps the first-ever guitar to be aimed squarely at the blues market. Guild guitars are no longer made in Westerly, Rhode Island, but the tradition is kept alive by Fender, who purchased the company in 1995.

above > **A classic cherry-red single-cutaway Guild Starfire III with a factory Bigsby. The single-coil DeArmond pickups ran from 1960 until 1963.**

right > **Mississippi John Hurt played Gibson and Guild flat-tops through the 1960s.**

blues guilds

The subtle, remarkably deft fingerpicker Mississippi John Hurt was first recorded in 1928. He used to play a guitar called Black Annie, its make and age unknown, but when he re-emerged onto the folk scene in 1963 Hurt didn't even possess his own instrument. After borrowing a number of guitars—including a Gibson J-45 and a Dobro—he chose a Guild F-30, paid for by the Newport Folk Festival, and subsequently appearing in Guild's promo literature in the 1960s. Guild electrics, meanwhile, were used by a number of blues artists including Buddy Guy. One of Guy's best-loved guitars through the 1970s and 1980s was a double-cutaway Starfire in a natural mahogany finish. Though this was Guild's take on Gibson's hugely successful ES-335, the company's own humbuckers gave the Starfire a unique voice all its own. Buddy Guy also endorsed the Guild Nighthawk solidbody, but returned to Stratocasters full-time in the 1990s.

identifier

guild's starfire

Launched in 1960, the single-cutaway versions, with laminated maple or mahogany bodies with single-coils, gained a bound back in 1962 and swapped over to humbuckers in 1963.

starfire I Single pickup model with harp tailpiece and dot-inlay rosewood board, in green, amber, or ebony finishes; discontinued 1964.

starfire II As Starfire I but with two pickups. Rosewood bridge replaces metal AjustoMatic type in 1973. Discontinued 1976.

starfire III As Starfire II but with Bigsby vibrato.

In 1964 the double-cutaway Starfires were launched with humbuckers as standard. The necks were made longer in 1967, joining at the 18th instead of the 16th fret, and a master volume control and block fingerboard inlays were introduced in 1973. Though all discontinued at various times, some models are still in production.

starfire IV The Buddy Guy model: two pickups, chrome hardware. Stopped in 1987, but now being made again.

starfire V As IV but with Guild/Bigsby vibrato. Last examples 1973.

starfire VI Top model with gold-plated hardware, Guild/Bigsby vibrato, and fancy inlays on an ebony board. Discontinued 1979.

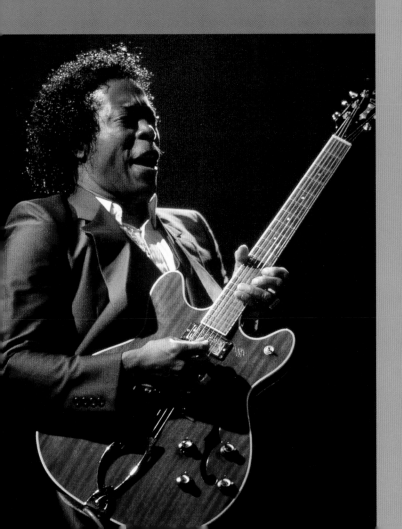

left > **Buddy Guy tears it up on his Guild Starfire in London in 1989.**

discography

A selective discography of the guitar players featured in this book.

Luther Allison >
Luther's Blues / 1974 / Gordy
Love Me Papa / 1977 / Evidence
Soul Fixin' Man / 1994 / Alligator

Eric Bibb >
Good Stuff / 1997 / Opus 3
Me to You / 1997 / Code Blue
Painting Signs / 2001 / Ruf 1071

Scrapper Blackwell >
Virtuoso guitar 1925-1934 /
    1925-1934 / Yazoo
Blue Before Sunrise / 1962 / 77

Blind Blake >
Complete Recorded Works, Vols. 1–4 /
    1926–1932 / Document
Ragtime Guitar's Foremost Fingerpicker /
    1926–1932 / Yazoo

Big Bill Broonzy >
The Young Big Bill Broonzy (1928–35) /
    1928–1935 / Yazoo
Good Time Tonight / 1930–1940 /
    Columbia/Legacy
Blues in the Mississippi Night / 1946 /
    Rykodisc
Big Bill's Blues / 1988 / Portrait

Clarence "Gatemouth" Brown >
The Original Peacock Recordings /
    1948–1959 / Rounder
Just Got Lucky / 1973 / Evidence
Pressure Cooker / 1973 / Alligator
Alright Again! / 1981 / Rounder
Texas Swing / 1988 / Rounder
Standing My Ground / 1989 / Alligator

R. L. Burnside >
Bad Luck City / 1991 / Fat Possum
Too Bad Jim / 1994 / Fat Possum
Rollin Tumblin / 1998 / Bong Load

Eric Clapton >
Eric Clapton / 1970 / Polydor
461 Ocean Boulevard / 1974 / Polydor
Slowhand / 1977 / Polydor
Money and Cigarettes / 1983 / Reprise
Crossroads / 1988 / Polydor
From the Cradle / 1994 / Reprise

Eric Clapton with Cream >
Disraeli Gears / 1967 / Polydor
Wheels of Fire / 1968 / Polydor

Albert Collins >
The Cool Sound of Albert Collins / 1965 /
Ice Pickin' / 1978 / Alligator
The Complete Imperial Recordnings / 1991 /
    EMI

Robert Cray >
Who's been Talkin' / 1980 / Atlantic
Bad Influence / 1983 / Hightone
Strong Persuader / 1986 / Mercury
Shame + a Sin / 1993 / Mercury

Cedell Davis >
Feelin like Doin' Something Wrong / 1994 /
    Fat Possum
The Best of Cedell Davis / 1995 / Fat Possum

Reverend Gary Davis >
Say No to the Devil / 1958 / Bluesville
At Newport / 1959 / Vanguard
Gospel, Blues & Street Songs / 1961 /
    Riverside

Blind Boy Fuller >
Truckin' My Blues Away / 1978 / Yazoo
East Coast Piedmont Style / 1991 /
Columbia/Legacy

Lowell Fulson >
Hung Down Dead / 1954 / MCA/Chess
Soul / 1966 / United
Everyday I Have the Blues / 1984 / Night Train
San Francisco Blues / 1988 / Black Lion

Guitar Slim >
Sufferin' Mind / 1991 / Specialty
Carolina Blues NYC 1944 / 1997 / Arhoolie

Buddy Guy >
I Left My Blues in San Francisco / 1968 /
    Chess
A Man and His Blues / 1968 / Vanguard
Damn Right, I've Got the Blues / 1991 /
    Silvertone
Slippin' In / 1994 / Silvertone

John Hammond >
Big City Blues / 1964 / Vanguard
Country Blues / 1964 / Vanguard
Hot tracks / 1978 / Vanguard
Live / 1983 / Rounder

Ben Harper >
Welcome to the Cruel Word / 1993 / Virgin
Fight for Your Mind / 1995 / Virgin
The Will to Live / Virgin / 1997
Burn to Shine / Virgin / 1999
With My Own Two Hands / 2003 / Virgin

Slim Harpo >
Rainin' in My Heart / 1961 / Excello
Scratch My Back: The best of Slim Harpo /
    1989 / Rhino

Jimi Hendrix >
Are You Experienced? / 1967 / MCA
Axis: Bold as Love / 1967 / MCA
Electric Ladyland / 1968 / MCA
Band of Gypsies / 1970 / Capitol

Earl Hooker >
Two Bugs and a Roach / 1966 / Arhoolie
Leading Brand / 1978 / Red Lightnin'
Blues Guitar / 1981 / Paula/Flyright

John Lee Hooker >
That's My Story/John Lee Hooker Sings the
    Blues / 1960 / Riverside
I'm John Lee Hooker / 1960 / Vee-Jay
John Lee Hooker Plays and Sings the Blues /
    1961 / MCA/Chess
John Lee Hooker at Newport / 1964 /
    Vee-Jay
Get Back Home / 1969 / Evidence
Boogie Chillun / 1972 / Fantasy

Son House >
Masters of the Delta Blues: The Friends of
    Charley Patton / 1930 / Yazoo
The Legendary Son House: Father of the Folk
    Blues / 1965 / Columbia

Howlin' Wolf >
The Real Folk Blues / 1966 / MCA/Chess
More Real Folk Blues / 1967 / MCA/Chess
Cadillac Daddy / 1989 / Rounder
Howlin' Wolf Rides Again / 1993 / Flair/Virgin

Mississippi John Hurt >
Avalon Blues / 1963 / Rounder
Worried Blues / 1963 / Rounder
Last Sessions / 1966 / Vanguard
Avalon Blues: The Complete 1928 OKeh
    recordings / 1996 / Sony

John Jackson >
Blues and Country Dance Tunes from
    Virginia / 1965 / Arhoolie
Don't Let Your Deal Go Down / 1970 /
    Arhoolie
Step It up & Go / 1979 / Rounder

Elmore James >
Whose Muddy Shoes / 1969 / MCA/Chess
The Original Meteor & Flair Sides / 1984 / Ace
King of the Slide Guitar / 1992 /
    Warner Brothers

Blind Lemon Jefferson >
Blind Lemon Jefferson / 1961 / Milestone
King of the Country Blues / 1985 / Yazoo

Blind Willie Johnson >
Praise God I'm Satisfied / 1989 / Yazoo
Sweeter as the Years Go By / 1990 / Yazoo

Lonnie Johnson >
Blues & Ballads / 1960 / Bluesville
Idle Hours / 1961 / Bluesville
The Complete Folkways Recordings / 1967 /
    Smithsonian/Folkways
Blues by Lonnie Johnson / 1979 / Bluesville

Robert Johnson >
King of the Delta Blues Singers / 1966 /
    Columbia
King of the Delta blues Singers, Vol. 2 /
1970 / Columbia
The Complete Recordings / 1990 /
    Columbia/Legacy

Albert King >
The Big Blues / 1962 / King
Born Under a Bad Sign / 1967 / Stax
King of the Blues guitar / 1969 / Atlantic
I'll Play the Blues for You / 1972 / Stax

B. B. King >
Singin' the Blues / 1956 / Crown
Live at the Regal / 1965 / ABC/MCA
Completely Well / 1969 / MCA
Anthology of the Blues: B. B. King /
    1969 / Kent
Back in the Alley / 1970 / MCA
Live in Cook County Jail / 1971 /MCA
Great Moments with B. B. King / 1981 / MCA
Spotlight on Lucille / 1991 / Flair
Singin' the Blues/The Blues / 1992 / Flair
My Sweet little Angel / 1993 / Flair

Freddie King >
Let's Hide Away and Dance Away /
    1961 / King
A Bonanza of Instruments / 1965 / King

Leadbelly >
Convict Blues / 1935 / Aldabra
Leadbelly / 1935 / Columbia
Library of Congress Recordings / 1966 /
    Elektra
Leadbelly Sings Folk Songs / 1990
Alabama Bound / 1990 / RCA

Furry Lewis >
Shake 'Em on Down / 1972 / Fantasy
In His Prime (1927–1928) / 1988 / Yazoo

Mance Lipscomb >
Texas Sharecropper & Songster / 1960 /
    Arhoolie
You Got to Reap What You Sow / 1964 /
    Arhoolie

Taj Mahal >
Natch'l Blues / 1968 / Columbia
Happy Just to Be Like I Am / 1971 /
    Mobile Fidelity

Brownie McGee >
Brownie McGhee & Sonny Terry Sing /
    1958 / Smithsonian/Folkways
Back Country Blues/ 1958 / Savoy
Brownie's Blues / 1971 / Bluesville
The Complete Brownie McGee / 1994 /
    Columbia

Blind Willie McTell >
Atlanta Twelve String / 1949 / Atlantic
Last Session / 1960 / Bluesville
Pig 'n Whistle Red / 1993 / Biograph

Memphis Minnie >
Hoodoo Lady (1933–1937) / 1933–1937) /
    Columbia
Blues Classics by Memphis Minnie / 1965 /
    Blues Classics

Charley Patton >
Founder of the Delta Blues / 1969 / Yazoo
King of the Delta Blues / 1991 / Yazoo

Bonnie Raitt >
Give It Up / 1972 / Warner Brothers
Takin' My Time / 1973 / Warner Brothers
Green Light / 1982 / Warner Brothers
Nick of Time / 1989 / Capitol
Road Tested / 1995 / Capitol
Silver Lining / 2002 / Capitol

Jimmy Reed >
I'm Jimmy Reed / 1959 / Vee-Jay
The Best of the Blues / 1963 / Vee-Jay

Jimmy Rogers >
Sloppy Drunk / 1973 / Black & Blue
Chicago Bound / 1976 / MCA/Chess

Otis Rush >
This One's a Good Un / 1968 / Blue Horizon
Door to Door / 1970 / MCA/Chess

Johnny Shines >
Last Night's Dream / 1968 / Warner Brothers
Johnny Shines with Big Walter Horton /
    1969 / Testament

Tampa Red >
Tampa Red (1928–1942) / 1928–1942 /
    Story of the Blues
Don't Tampa with the Blues / 1961 / Prestige
Bottleneck Guitar (1928–1937) / 1974 /
    Yazoo
Tampa Red: Guitar Wizard / 1975 / RCA

Sister Rosetta Tharpe >
Sacred & Secular / 1941–1969 / Rosetta
Sister Rosetta Tharpe/The Sam Price Trio /
    1958 / Decca

Stevie Ray Vaughan >
Texas Flood / 1983 / Epic
Couldn't Stand the Weather / 1984 / Epic
Soul to Soul / 1985 / Epic
In Step / 1989 / Epic

T-Bone Walker >
T-Bone Blues / 1959 / Atantic
Singing the Blues / 1960 / Imperial

Muddy Waters >
First Recording Sessions 1941–1946 /
    1941–1946 / Document
At Newport / 1960 / MCA/Chess
Muddy Waters Sings Big Bill Broonzy /
    1964 / MCA/Chess
The Real Folk Blues / 1965 / MCA/Chess
More Real Folk Blues / 1967 / MCA/Chess
Woodstock Album / 1975 / Chess
Hard Again / 1977 / Blue Sky

Johnny "Guitar" Watson >
Gangster of Love / 1958 / Charly
Johnny Guitar Watson / 1963 / King

The White Stripes >
White Stripes / 1999 /
    Sympathy for the Record Industry
De Stijl / 2000 /
    Sympathy for the Record Industry
White Blood Cells / 2001 /
    Sympathy for the Record Industry/XL
Elephant / 2003 / V2 Records

Robert Pete Williams >
Angola Prisoner's Blues / 1961 / Arhoolie
Free Again / 1961 / Original Blues Calssics
I'm as Blue as a Man Can be / 1994 /
    Arhoolie

Johnny Winter >
Johnny Winter / 1969 / Columbia
Second Winter / 1969 / Columbia
Guitar Slinger / 1984 / Alligator
Live in NYC '97 / 1998 / Virgin

index

Figures in *italics* refer to captions; those in **bold** indicate main references.

credits

Quarto and the author would like to thank the following for their kind permission to reproduce their pictures:

(Key: l left, r right, t top, b bottom, c centre)

Pages 6, 7, 42 l, 42 r, 48, 49 c, 50, 51 bl, 51 br, 58 t, 60 b, 64 t, 66 t, 67 br, 74 t, 75 r, 76 t, 77 t, 91 br, 93 c, 94 t, 95 r, 96 t, 96 bl, 97 tr, 97 br, 98 t, 99 br, 100 t, 100 b, 104 t, 104 b, 106, 107 bl, 107 tr, 107 br, 108 l, 108 r, 109 tr, 110 t, 111 r, 112 t, 113 r, 114 t, 114 b, 115 bl, 115 r, 116 t, 117 lc, 118 t, 120 t, 121 tr, 121 br, 122 t, 123 r, 124, 125 r, 126, 128, 129 br, 130 t, 132 t, 136 t, 138 t, 140, 142 t, 143 r, 144 r, 148 t, 149 r, 150 t, 151 br, 152 t, 153 tr, 154 t, 154 bl, 155 tr, 156 t, 156 b, 158, 162 t, 162 b, 164, 166 t, 168 t, 170 b, 174 t, 178 t, 180 t, 182 t, 182 b, 184 t The Balafon Image Bank; 10 Peter Szego; 11 Nicky J. Sims / Redferns; 12 l, 13 br, 18-19 c Peter Newark's American Pictures; 12-13 c, 14, 20-21, 26, 30, 41 t, 41 b, 75 bl, 110 b, 123 bl, 127 bl, 129 bl, 160, 179 b, 184 b Michael Ochs Archives / Redferns; 15, 24 t, 49 bl, 118 b, 168 b Pictorial Press; 16 The Western Collection / Sylvia Pitcher Photo Library; 17, 77 bl Julie Snow / Frank Driggs Collection; 18 tl John Hurt / Redferns; 18 bl Fred Mc Dowell / Redferns; 22, 23, 25 t, 29, 39, 40, 44, 53 bl, 55 l, 57, 59 bl, 61 bl, 67 bl, 69 bl, 79 bl, 84 b, 85 bl, 98 bl, 111 bl, 113 b, 120 br, 121 bl, 130 bl, 180 bl, 180-181 bc Frank Driggs Collection; 24 b Max Jones Files / Redferns; 25 b, 27 t, 28 l Ray Flerlage / Frank Driggs Collection; 27 b Glen A. Baker Archives / Redferns; 28 tr Brian Shuel / Redferns; 28 br, 31, 89 bl, 119 b, 134, 137 br, 138 b, 139 br, 145 b, 157 b, 172 b, 185 b David Redfern / Redferns; 32 Kelly Joe Phelps / Redferns; 33 t Robin Little / Redferns; 33 b Brigitte Engl / Redferns; 36 r (1932) Sears Brands, LLC; 37 l, 72 c, 72 r, 73 r, 74 b, 77 br, 78 l, 79 tr, 79 br, 80 l, 80 tr, 81 r, 82 t, 82 bl, 83 bl, 83 tr, 83 br, 84 t, 85 r, 176 t, 176 b Colin McCubbin; 37 r, 105 r, 109 br, 131 r, 163 r, 170 r, 172 t Guitar Magazine; 36 l, 52 r, 54 t, 55 r, 56, 59 tr, 59 br, 60 t, 61 tr, 61 br, 68 t, 70, 167 br, Courtesy of Paul Brett / Photography Dewi Wyn; 43, 132 br, 154 br, 167 bl, 169 b, 183 b Tom Copi / Frank Driggs Collection; 45 t, 94 b, 117 r, 141 r, 147 b, 151 tr, 153 br, 175 r Gibson Guitar Corp; 45 b, 73 bl, 87 tr, 87br, 88 t National Reso-Phonic Guitars, Inc.; 49 r, 178 b, 181 r Courtesy of C.F Martin & Co; 52 l (1927) Sears Brands, LLC; 62-63 Jim Chappelle / Frank Driggs Collection; 65 b Martin Philbey / Redferns; 66 b Universal Music Group, (Released on the Mercury Label, Recorded 1964); 71 Deltahaze Corporation / Redferns; 72 l, 76 bl, 76 br USPTO; 78 br Universal Music Group, (Recorded 1962, Cover Photo by Paul Oliver); 78 tr Geoff Dann / Redferns; 80 br From the Arhoolie CD 323 © Arhoolie Productions Inc. USA. www.arhoolie.com.

Photographer Kelly Hart. Use by permission, all rights reserved; 81 bl Joe Alper / Frank Driggs Collection; 86, 88 bl, 92 l, 125 bl, 153 bl Ebet Roberts / Redferns; 87 bl Leon Morris / Redferns; 88 br Simon Ritter / Redferns; 90-91 c Charles B. Nadell / Frank Driggs Collection; 92-93 c Escott / Pictorial Press; 95 bl, 155 bl, 171 b Sylvia Pitcher Photo Library; 96-97 c Eugene Washington / Bill Greensmith Collection / Juke Blues Magazine; 101 b Steve Cropper / Redferns; 102 Universal Music Group, (Released on the Chess Label, recorded 1960, Cover Design + Photo by Don Bronstein);103 Ian Dickson / Redferns; 105 bl Susan Moore / Redferns; 109 bl Mick Hutson / Redferns; 112 b, 141 bl, Gems / Redferns; 116-117 bc, 144 l, 163 bl Chuck Boyd / Redferns; 116 br Harry Goodwin / Redferns; 120 bl Universal Music Group, (Released on the Chess Label, Recorded 1964, Cover Design by Nachtow / Bronstein); 130-131 bc Elliott Landy / Redferns; 132 bl Fin Costello / Redferns; 133 b, 146-147 t James Dittiger / Redferns; 135 Robert Knight / Redferns; 136 b Ann Stern / Redferns; 137 bl, 139 bl Richie Aaron / Redferns; 142-143 bc Paul Natkin / Photo Reserve / Guitar Magazine; 148 bl President Records, (Recorded 1968, Cover Photo by Nashboro Records); 148-149 bc Showtime / Pictorial Press; 150 c Universal Music Group, (Released on the Chess Label, Recorded 1966, Cover Photo by Don Bronstein); 150 b Universal Music Group, (Released on the Chess Label, Recorded 1961, Cover Design + Photo by Don Bronstein); 151 bl PP / Tony Gale / Pictorial Press; 152 bl Henrietta Butler / Redferns; 159 b Robert Barclay / Frank Driggs Collection; 161 b Mike Rowe / Pictorial Press; 165 bl From the Arhoolie CD 468 © Arhoolie Productions Inc.; USA. www.arhoolie.com. Photographer Harry Chris Strachwitz. Use by permission, all rights reserved; 165 br Graham Wiltshire / Redferns; 166 b From the Arhoolie CD 394 © Arhoolie Productions Inc. USA. www.arhoolie.com. Photographer Harry Oster. Use by permission, all rights reserved; 173 b Patrick Ford / Redferns; 174 bl From the Arhoolie CD 9026 © Arhoolie Productions Inc. USA. www.arhoolie.com. Photographer Jim Crockett. Use by permission, all rights reserved; 174-175 bc Robert Tilling ; 177 b Jon Super / Redferns.

While every effort has been made by Quarto and the author to contact and duly credit all authors, artists and original copyright holders of material appearing in this book. We apologize in advance for any omissions or errors, and would be grateful to receive notification of such so that we may correct this information in future editions.